A

MW01672394

AND

RECOVERY

Solving the mystery of reunion

Evelyn Burns Robinson

Clova Publications

Published by

Clova Publications
PO Box 328
Christies Beach
South Australia 5165
www.clovapublications.com

Copyright © Evelyn Robinson 2004

This book is copyright. Apart from any fair dealing for the purposes of private study, research, criticism or review, as permitted under the Copyright Act, no part may be reproduced by any process without written permission. Inquiries should be addressed to the publisher.

ISBN 978-0-9871931-1-7

First published in Australia in 2004
Reprinted in 2006 & 2011

By the same author:

Adoption and Loss – *The Hidden Grief*

Adoption Reunion – *Ecstasy or Agony?*

Adoption Separation - *Then and now*

~~~~~~
~~~~~~

This book is dedicated to my five children. Each one of them has taught me different lessons and brought different gifts into my life.

A Tear and a Smile

I would not exchange the sorrows of my heart for the joys of the multitude. And I would not have the tears that sadness makes to flow from my every part, turn into laughter. I would that my life remain a tear and a smile.

A tear to unite me with those of broken heart; a smile to be a sign of my joy in existence.

Kahlil Gibran

CONTENTS

Introduction

Who am I?

I am a mother who was separated for twenty-one years from my first child, after he was adopted. His name is Stephen and he was born in Scotland in 1970. When Stephen was nineteen years old, I joined a post-adoption support organisation for mothers separated from their children by adoption and was involved with that organisation for fifteen years. During that time I spoke with many people who had experienced separation from a family member through adoption and with many others working in the post-adoption field.

Because of the experience I had gained, both in my life and through my voluntary work with the support organisation, I decided to return to study in 1995 and completed a post-graduate degree in social work. Throughout my professional studies, I explored grief and loss issues and how these applied to adoption. I was then employed as Counsellor/Co-ordinator for four years by the support organisation in which I had worked for many years as a volunteer. My principal client group consisted of mothers who had been separated from their children through adoption, although I also counselled others affected by adoption separation. I later provided my counselling services privately.

In my first book, *Adoption and Loss - The Hidden Grief*, I told of my experience of becoming pregnant, of being separated from my son by adoption and of my reunion with Stephen when he was twenty-one years old. I also explored the on-going impact which the separation from my son had had on my life. From a professional perspective, I explored the meaning of adoption separation and the grief which follows that separation.

I should like to express my appreciation to all of those who felt moved, after reading my first book, to share their thoughts and experiences with me.

My travels in 2001

At the end of March, 2001 I left my home in Australia and travelled for three months, speaking at conferences and public meetings in New Zealand, the United States, Canada, England, the Republic of Ireland, Scotland and Northern Ireland. During these three months, I covered more than thirty thousand miles and fulfilled twenty-one speaking engagements. I addressed audiences totalling more than one thousand people. Approximately half of that number were professionals who were providing post-adoption services for adults who had been involved in adoption separations.

I talked with some very knowledgeable and understanding professionals on my travels. Sadly, however, many of those working with adults in the post-adoption area seemed to have little understanding of grief and loss issues for those affected by adoption separation and offered little support for those who wished to contact adult family members from whom they had been separated. Others were aware of the issues, but unfortunately constrained by resource limitations and legislative restrictions.

I have wonderful memories of people and places and I thoroughly enjoyed every moment of my trip, which took me literally around the world. It was very interesting and informative for me to hear the views and attitudes of those providing post-adoption services in other countries, as well as listening to those with a personal experience of adoption.

I know, because many of those whom I met on my travels have told me, that my presentations have had an impact and that changes are taking place in many locations. In every country that I visited, I met welcoming, generous people who were interested in what I had to say. The trip was a wonderful experience and I should like to thank all of those who shared not only their homes and their time with me on my travels, but also their views and their experiences. I am also grateful to the many people who heard me speak and contacted me after I had returned to Australia.

During my trip, I asked questions, I answered questions, I talked and I listened. This book grew out of those discussions. I was asked at the end of one of my presentations, if I had ever been asked a question which I could not answer. I replied, that I had always been able to provide *an* answer to any question, but that I could not guarantee that I was able to provide *the* answer to every question.

One question I was asked frequently was how people could help themselves, when there was no appropriate professional assistance available. I have written this book in the hope that it will assist those who prefer to address their issues without seeking professional support and those who are unable to access appropriate services. In addition, I believe that it presents a valuable complement to any professional counselling which is undertaken. I know that this book will also be of great value to professionals working in a therapeutic setting with adult family members who have been separated by adoption.

Since 2001, I have continued to travel and share my views on adoption loss and recovery, in my own time and at my own expense. I have never charged a fee for speaking. The interactions which I have had in recent years with members of the adoption community around the world and with interested professionals have reinforced my beliefs in the ways in which healing can be achieved through understanding and experiencing adoption loss.

About *Adoption and Recovery*

The title *Adoption and Recovery* refers to two types of recovery from the separation created by adoption. Firstly, adoption separation causes an emotional trauma for those affected and I believe that an emotional *recovery* will help to heal the pain of the losses associated with adoption separation. The connection between the physical body and the emotional self is complex. I have often witnessed how people's physical well-being improves as they begin to address their emotional issues. The two are closely intertwined and in the same way that physical pain indicates that an area of the body needs treatment, so emotional pain indicates that there are issues which require attention, in order that we can recover and feel emotionally well again. I have termed this 'personal recovery'. *Personal recovery is about addressing the effects of adoption separation on individuals.*

Secondly, when something is lost and then found, it is often said to have been *recovered.* When an adoption takes place, a child and his or her families of origin are separated from each other. This separation means that losses are experienced. When family members who have been separated from each other by adoption find each other again and are reunited, therefore, they are, in a sense, *recovering* each other. This can be an opportunity to develop the relationships which were interrupted by the adoption. I have termed this 'interpersonal recovery'. *Interpersonal recovery is about addressing the effects of adoption separation on the relationships between family members.*

The title of this book, therefore, refers to the dual meaning of the word *recovery* and includes both personal and interpersonal recovery. I have been privileged to witness the transformation which recovery in both senses of the word brings to people's lives. I should like to express my admiration for all of those who have shown the courage to attempt to achieve both personal and interpersonal recovery. For those who have not yet done so, I hope that this book will encourage them along that pathway.

In Part I of this book, I describe the journey from adoption separation, through the experience of mourning that separation towards a place of personal recovery. In Part II of this book, I describe the journey from adoption reunion, through managing the grief which often accompanies reunion, towards a place of interpersonal recovery.

In *Adoption and Loss – The Hidden Grief*, I outlined my personal journey through adoption separation, personal recovery and interpersonal recovery. In *Adoption and Recovery – Solving the mystery of reunion*, I have used a selection from the questions which I have been asked over the years, to illustrate the insights which I have gained into adoption separation and the recovery process. In Part III of this book, I have provided an interesting and varied selection of those questions and my responses to them. Any identifying details have been altered or removed. The issues surrounding adoption reunion seem to have puzzled academics and researchers for many years. Hopefully these questions and answers will shed some much-needed light on the subject.

I conclude this book by exploring the implications of my understanding of adoption recovery, both personal and interpersonal, for our governments, for our communities and for us as individuals.

The mystery of reunion

The sub-title of this book, *Solving the mystery of reunion*, refers to the fact that many adults who have been separated from family members by adoption, professionals working with those people, members of the general community and also legislators seem to be, to a large extent, baffled by adoption reunions. They struggle to understand the reasons behind the desire of family members who have been separated by adoption to reunite and also the issues which arise for them when they do. I believe that in explaining the concept of adoption recovery, both on a personal and on an interpersonal level, I have been able to solve both of these 'mysteries'.

It is my view that so many have failed to comprehend the events surrounding adoption reunions, because there has been a vital piece of information which has been missing. That information is, that the reunion experience itself is an important part of the adoption grieving process. Once that missing detail is supplied, many people's reunion experiences make sense and the mystery of reunion is solved.

It has gradually become clear to me over the years that, although reunion often brings great joy into people's lives, many of the experiences of adoption reunion which people have described to me and about which I have read, are remarkably similar to the experiences of those who are grieving a bereavement. If you read reports by those who have been involved in adoption reunions, you will read of much grief. It may not be recognised or identified by the participants as grief, but you will read of tears, anger, numbness, a sense of loss, disorientation, sadness, fear and guilt. All of these are components of grieving.

If you have never considered that the experience of reunion is a grieving experience, then I suggest that you read those accounts again with this in mind and you may be able to identify those reactions as being grieving responses. As a result of giving this matter serious consideration, I have found an explanation for the significance of the reunion experience which satisfies me. Through listening, reading and applying my professional knowledge, I believe that I have come to an understanding of what is happening in the lives of those who have been motivated to seek an adoption reunion and what actually occurs when an adoption reunion takes place.

Anecdotal evidence suggests that parents who have lost children through adoption and also adopted people are over-represented as clients in mental health care. I believe that this has occurred because their loss and grief experiences have not been recognised or addressed. Grief itself is not a mental health issue. Grieving is an appropriate and useful response to a loss. I believe that too often the lack of understanding of the need to grieve adoption losses has led to inappropriate responses to what is, in fact, grieving behaviour. I hope that this book will help to educate the community to recognise and acknowledge adoption loss and grief.

My first book focussed on the losses experienced by those affected by adoption separation and the grief which results from those losses. This book focuses on the experiences of those who are striving to work through that grief towards both personal and interpersonal recovery and the part played in the recovery process by the reunion experience. Many books have been written about adoption reunions, but *Adoption and Recovery – Solving the mystery of reunion* is unique. ***This is the first book to explain the dynamics of adoption reunion within a grief framework.***

Sadly, in many parts of the world, the concept of adoption recovery is not recognised or understood and so post-adoption services for adults who have experienced an adoption separation, *if they exist at all*, have evolved in a social climate characterised by an ignorance of adoption loss and grief. Because of this, those services are unlikely to be appropriate or useful. To illustrate the importance of understanding the true nature of the situation before devising a suitable response, I should like to relate an experience from my youth.

I have always enjoyed Scottish country dancing. When I was fifteen years old, I was participating, one Saturday evening, in a lively eightsome reel, when I fell backwards and landed on my left wrist. My wrist hurt, but I continued to dance for the remainder of the evening as best I could. When I arrived home I told my mother about my accident. My mother studied my swollen wrist, considered the contents of her medicine cabinet and decided that the application of some *Deep Heat* to the affected area would be an appropriate treatment.

I tried to sleep, but the pain kept me awake. I woke my mother during the night complaining of the pain in my wrist. Further applications of *Deep Heat* followed, until the burning from the supposedly soothing balm was actually causing more discomfort to me than the original injury. Sleep was impossible.

The next day I carried on stoically about my business, until finally I felt that I needed a professional diagnosis. I attended the emergency department of the nearest hospital in the afternoon and arrived home that evening with my left arm in plaster. The x-rays had shown that my wrist was broken.

My mother had done her best to treat my pain with the limited skills, equipment and information which were available to her. However, it was only when my problem was presented to someone who had greater skills and more sophisticated equipment and was therefore able to obtain the crucial information which allowed an accurate diagnosis, that my injury was treated in an appropriate manner, which led to healing.

Similarly, post-adoption services for adults who have been separated from family members because of adoption, will not be useful or appropriate until those responsible for such services are aware of the true nature of the underlying issues.

The value of qualitative data

It certainly was not my intention, when, in 1989, I first became involved with post-adoption services, to begin collecting material for a qualitative study on the significance of the adoption reunion experience. Since that time, however, I have informally collected data from many people whose lives have been affected by adoption and from professionals and volunteers working in the post-adoption field.

In this book, I have documented the conclusions which I have reached after considering those data and reflecting on them. Those conclusions are informed by my personal experience of adoption separation and reunion and underpinned by my extensive professional knowledge and experience as a social worker and counsellor. I appreciate all of those who have shared their feelings and experiences with me, in whatever form that sharing has occurred. They have all helped to enlighten me.

Although I have not included a literature review in this book, as I did in *Adoption and Loss – The Hidden Grief*, I acknowledge that my conclusions about adoption separation and reunion have also been influenced by many of the books and articles which I have read over the last fifteen years.

I know that there are many people who experience the emotions which I have described. I am aware that they exist in great numbers and, for that reason, their experiences deserve to be considered. My intention in writing this book is to speak *to* all of those who have been separated from family members by adoption. I do not claim to speak *for* all of those who have found themselves in that position.

I should like to express my appreciation to everyone who contributed to this book in any way; to those who have shared their experiences and emotions with me and to those who have encouraged and assisted me to offer my views to the community in the form of writing and publishing this book.

Explanation of terms

When a person who was adopted as a child meets his or her mother, a reunion takes place. Whether or not the mother ever saw or held the child, they were intimately connected before their separation. When those who have been adopted meet other family members, such as fathers, siblings and grandparents, this may be a reunion, if there was an original meeting, or it may be that they are meeting for the first time. In order to avoid repeating this fact, I have, on occasion, used the word *reunion* in this book to refer to the meetings between those who have been adopted and their family members, whether or not those meetings were actually reunions in the technical sense.

The reunions referred to in this book are meetings which occur after the adopted person has reached adulthood. A reunion is an actual meeting, although this may be preceded by contact by telephone, letter or exchange of information through an intermediary.

To avoid confusion, I have chosen in this book to refer to the parents who physically created the children who were subsequently adopted, as the *parents*, or as the *mothers* and *fathers* of the children. I refer to those who adopted the children as the *adopters*, or as the *adoptive mothers* and *adoptive fathers*. *Adopters* is the term which appears on the legal birth certificate of my son, Stephen.

I use the term *relatives* to refer to those who are related by blood and not to those who are related by law. I have described those who are adopted as *adopted persons*. However, to avoid the unwieldy *adult adopted persons*, I have, on occasion, used the term *adopted adults* to refer to those who were adopted as children and are now adults. When a child is born, he or she becomes a member of two families, the family of the mother and the family of the father. I refer in this book, therefore, to the adopted person's original *families*.

In matters of addressing grief, I have referred to books by two authors who are recognised as authorities on grief and grief counselling. They are: *Grief Counselling and Grief Therapy*, by J. William Worden (Revised Edition, 1991) and *The Anatomy of Bereavement*, by Beverley Raphael (1983).

Adoption in our lives

In the families into which they are born, many children have grandparents, aunts, uncles, cousins and siblings. Family membership has several aspects. There are legal relationships in a family, but there are also physical and emotional relationships. Adoption dissolves the legal relationships between the child and the members of the families of origin, but not the physical relationships.

For many parents, it also does not dissolve the emotional relationships. Because adopted people usually have no conscious memory of their original families, however, they may not be aware of an emotional relationship, until they have the opportunity to develop this as adults. Sometimes, therefore, when reunion occurs, they are surprised by the depth of their emotions.

Statistics for Australia, New Zealand, the United States of America, Canada, the United Kingdom and the Republic of Ireland show that adopted people make up approximately two per cent of the population. Based on these figures, it is likely that approximately one quarter of the population has had a close relationship with an adopted person. Books such as this, therefore, are of interest to a great many people.

Many fascinating accounts of family reunions have already been published, which are evidence that just because family members are separated from each other, this does not mean that they do not continue to care about and be interested in each other. Many of the issues faced by family members separated by adoption are also faced by family members separated for other reasons. I am confident that this book will be valuable, not only to those who have experienced family separation, but also to professionals who are working with them.

I have no doubt that those who have experienced an adoption separation will eventually succeed, with the support of professionals, in making governments around the world aware of their responsibilities. I believe that legislation allowing equal rights to access identifying information to adopted adults and their mothers (as well as other family members, where appropriate) will be passed in the near future in many places. I also believe that the provision of appropriate counselling, searching and information services will accompany such legislation. This is an issue of social justice, which urgently needs to be addressed.

Many people have asked my advice about their personal situations, especially in relation to reunions. What I am hoping is that this book will give people a better understanding of why they feel the way that they do about the presence of adoption in their lives and why certain issues have arisen for them during adoption reunions. I believe that it will then be easier for them to be in touch with their own feelings around adoption and also to empathise with the other parties involved.

My aim in writing this book is not to provide universal solutions to the outcomes experienced by those who have been separated by adoption, but to help them to understand their experiences, so that they can then discover and implement their own solutions.

A message from my son, Stephen

My name is Stephen Miller Ferguson. I was born in Edinburgh, Scotland in 1970 and was given to my new family 6 days later. I have since been reunited with my mother and siblings, who now all live in Australia. Here are my thoughts on growing up with adoption and the importance of reunion.

I have many fond memories of my childhood: the family holidays to Rothesay, kissing girls, meeting granny on a summer's day, playing football on the grass at the end of my street and long walks with the dog. The noting of depression was a blip on an otherwise happy-go-lucky, early childhood.

Apparently I was depressed enough in school as a 5 year old to warrant it being noted by my classroom teacher and written on my report card. My parents said that they enquired at the time as to my state of mind, but I apparently conveyed to them that nothing was wrong, as much as a 5 year old is able to.

I excelled at school for many years after such a seemingly gloomy start. I was deemed the second most intelligent child in my whole school when I was 11 and it was even suggested that I would be able to skip a year in High School and go into a class with children a year ahead of me academically. School was easy and enjoyable for me and I had many friends there. I must have been a joy for my adoptive parents, more than they could have dreamed of. I was good-looking, popular and friendly. I did school plays, Burns poetry recitals, solo-singing and Scottish country dancing displays.

My life seemed completely unaffected by the knowledge that I had originally come from another family – in fact I don't think it really came into my thinking at all, except for the regular episodes of self-discipline in the bathroom, away from prying eyes and inquisitive parents, that I inflicted on myself around the age of 7 or 8. It was as if I had a split personality, that when I stepped into that bathroom, I turned into a bad little boy that deserved to be bent over the side of the bath and smacked. Out of the bathroom I was my usual, cheerful self.

Did I think of myself as bad because I had been given away? It always felt like a subconscious thing, something that was buried deep inside of me that only surfaced on occasion. It may have been that something triggered those episodes, but my memory is failing me on that point. It is possible, however, that I am suppressing the information – who knows? All I know is that somewhere around 10 years old, it stopped.

I grew up with another strange quirk other than the self-spanking. I rocked myself to sleep on a regular basis, sometimes quite violently, right up until I was in my mid-20s. Was I secretly missing my mother?

My adoptive parents did a good thing telling me from an early age that I had been born from another mother. That meant that I grew up in a truthful life, not one soiled by family secrets, hypocrisy and on-going deception. I do remember going to collect my adopted younger brother when I was 4 years old, with the words, "We're going to get you a brother today", ringing in my ears. We went to a house with a woman and some children in the living room. My new 'brother', David, as he was later renamed, was sitting in his pram in the middle of the room. We picked him up and left, our instant family member in tow, as we bussed it back home.

Even at 4 years old I thought this to be strange. I played with him the same as any young sibling would and we fought often, as blood-related brothers do, but he never *felt* like my brother, not really. He was called my brother and I told everyone he was my brother, but he never truly *felt* like my brother. I couldn't have qualified what 'feeling like my brother' was actually like, but I just knew that the inherent closeness I often saw experienced by natural siblings was missing from my relationship with David. It always has been and as our lives head off in different directions, I know that it always will be.

I find the whole 'name-changing' part of adoption to be slightly uncomfortable. When you are renamed, your original identity is over-written and you are forced to grow up as someone else, someone new. This is not the choice of the person whose starting point in life has been hidden from the rest of the world and I think it is a popular misconception of adoptive parents that if they 'just erase all traces of former identity and replace them with a new family name' then everything will be great and the child will grow up not thinking about their mother or father. I don't think it is fair on the adopted person to do this and I am eternally grateful to the legislators who decided that the original birth certificate of the adopted person was to be kept and that the new certificate must be stamped with the word 'ADOPTED' at the top of it. This enabled me to trace my first name and therefore the woman who carried me for 40 weeks, then gave birth to me and all the history that goes with that.

I have been and still am to date, fighting for people created by donor sperm to have their true origins stamped on their birth certificates too. It helps to reduce the potential for secrets and lies. Being adopted and a sperm donor I am in the unique position of seeing this clearly from both sides.

The thought of reunion was a fuzzy distant one early on. I didn't start to think deeply about my natural family until I was in my mid-teens. As I was growing up and my face was changing into more like the one I have now, I began to be more acutely aware of the glaring differences between how my parents looked and how I looked. We were also growing in different directions mentally too, but that's another story.

It never ceased to amaze me how, when people see parents with a child and that child is identified as their son, they automatically remark how much he looks like parent A or parent B. I'm not sure if they actually look closely before they open their mouths or notice the difference, but dare not open the can of worms that potentially something along the blunt lines of, "He looks nothing like either of you, how come he's your son?" would open. Then my brother started growing up and not looking like anyone else either. Again strangers would comment, "Don't you and your brother look so alike?" I always wanted to say, "Are you blind or just pretending to be? We look nothing like each other!", but the ensuing trouble that would have erupted, had I uttered those impetuous words was enough to stop me in my tracks.

Puberty hit late and with it I was more determined to find out what was beneath the increasingly flimsy façade of where I came from. I have no recollection of my adoptive parents ever discussing anything in-depth about my adoption with me as I was growing up, or offering to nudge me in the direction of my natural family. They later said that they had left everything to me and that if I had ever approached them, then they would have gladly helped me. I don't think my adoptive parents ever liked the idea that I was so open about where I came from. It possibly hurt them to have me remind everyone that one of them, for some reason or other, couldn't have children the natural way.

The desire to search was there, but I kept it suppressed for years, until I had the right circumstances in which to start. Privacy was my main concern at this point. There was a very good chance that this would turn out to be quite an explosive journey I was about to embark on and I needed a bit of space for myself, away from family interference and friendly distractions. To me 'wanting to know where you came from' and 'needing to fill in the genetic gaps' is completely natural and needs no explanation. In fact, I never hear of anyone questioning people who trace their own blood-related family history – why should we as adopted people always have to justify *our* search? And why do so many people automatically think that there must be something wrong with our current family life that spurs us to seek out our own blood-related family members?

Adopted people are living in an artificially created family environment with new names and identities given to us by strangers. It may well be a loving and stable relationship, but that shouldn't necessarily negate any of those feelings of wanting to seek out your mother, father and/or brothers and sisters. Looking for a reunion certainly does not indicate anything wrong with one's adoptive family. I think the issues are unrelated. A reunion is a step forward in self-awareness. It is a way of truly getting to know yourself and accepting that your origins are different from what you see surrounding you in the family home. There is nothing wrong with feeling like that and in my opinion it would do more harm than good, if those feelings were suppressed and buried. How much more damage is done psychologically to people, when they are told they are betraying their adoptive parents, for wanting to do the most natural thing they know? Forced guilt is a terrible way to control people.

As a society it would be better if we fostered openness, honesty and respect by actively encouraging adopted people to search for their natural heritage. To deny people the opportunity to reunite with the woman and/or man that created them, is plainly wrong.

My reunion happened in 1991.

Evelyn and I had been using the exact same person to try to contact each other, from opposite sides of the globe, at the same time. Call it coincidence. Call it spiritual bond between mother and son. I call it serendipity. However I can't express enough how deeply touched I was to know that my mother was busy searching for me, her first son, at exactly the same time I was searching for her. It gave me a sense of belonging. I was wanted, again. I suppose adopted people like myself who don't openly discuss 'growing up with adoption in their lives', with their adoptive parents will always wonder about the hows and whys of the day they were entrusted to an unknown family. They may go over in their minds, many times, the reasons and the circumstances as to why they are no longer with their mother and blood-relatives. I know I did. Again, I believe this to be a healthy symptom of natural curiosity. All of those unanswered questions, all of those musings and imaginings, answered in a positive light by one simple piece of information. We were going to be reunited and I was left in a sweet, contented daze.

For 6 months I had contacted Evelyn by letter and telephone. Soon after our first contact she sent me the money to buy a plane ticket to Australia and within 2 months of the cheque's arrival, I was there in person. Meeting her and my new blood-siblings (2 younger brothers and 2 younger sisters) was an enlightening and exhilarating experience for me. I suddenly felt the true value of family. I remember vividly coming out of the airport gate and seeing for the first time in my life, at 21 years of age, someone who genuinely looked like me. Actually there were 5 people who looked like me! I didn't feel so alone anymore.

I have to mention here for the record that Evelyn had in fact tried to contact me about 2 years previous to me finding her. The third party religious intermediary who was used in my adoption was asked to initiate contact with me. He first called my adoptive parents and told them that the mother was interested in making contact with the son and was given 2 things – some small pieces of general information about me and an angry warning, never to contact them again. I only found this out after I had made contact with Evelyn. To say I was disappointed in their behaviour is an understatement and has only served to complicate our relationship further.

This had lost me 2 more years.

Geography has played a big part in my reunion experience, making it slower than I would have liked. I have tried to visit Australia as often as my life allows and Evelyn has also been to see me in Scotland and Japan. Each time brings with it new understandings of who I am and where I stand in this big universe of ours.

It enriches my life and allows me to transcend the usual boundaries of family relationships. It bridges gaps and brings with it a multitude of exciting new opportunities for personal growth.

My adoptive parents appear to have now finally come round to a similar way of thinking. As I have grown and evolved, so too have they. At the beginning we seemed to be poles apart in our understanding of what it means to be adopted and the impact that can have on your life, but over the years they have slowly changed their views on the subject. I am relieved – it means we can all move forward as a family now instead of me swimming against the tide of their stubborn refusal to delve into my world. I have seen a new side to them and I have my reunion experience to thank for that.

Reunion with my natural, blood-related family members is an on-going process. It is one that I relish and one that adds countless precious moments to my life. I personally feel much more whole. I now have a fuller understanding of my origins and therefore of who I am.

I also know that the benefits reunion has bestowed upon Evelyn, my mother, are numerous and vitally important.

If I think about all the new people and interesting experiences I have had as a direct result of my reunion, I find it difficult to quantify. From the joy of meeting my family to the satisfaction of directly helping other adoptees meet theirs, to nieces and nephews and cousins and aunts and uncles and grandparents and brothers and sisters that I never knew I had, to a more complete interpretation of what makes me who I am in this world – I owe it all to 'reunion'.

Stephen Ferguson
March 2004

Part I
Personal Recovery

Chapter 1
Adoption Separation

What does it mean for those involved when a child is separated from his or her family by adoption?

The meaning of the pregnancy

In some societies, couples do not marry until a child has first of all been born to them. In some societies there is no marriage and all children are welcomed and celebrated in the same way. In many societies, however, there is the expectation that couples will not produce children until after they have been married. It is in such societies that children born out of wedlock are viewed as a problem. In some situations, the way to deal with that problem has been for the child to be removed from the family and adopted into another family. Many parents were taught that having a child out of wedlock was a social, if not a moral crime and that, in order to ensure that their children did not suffer as a result of their crime, they should agree to be separated from their children and for another couple to raise them. As a result, many children were removed from their families and adopted into families to whom they were not related.

Many mothers, therefore, experienced considerable emotional trauma, which began when their pregnancies were confirmed, continued through breaking the news of their pregnancies to family and friends, affected them throughout the duration of their pregnancies and at the time of birth and stayed with them for many years afterwards.

A more detailed study of the grief resulting from adoption separation and its long-term outcomes is provided in my first book, *Adoption and Loss – The Hidden Grief.*

Anticipatory grief

In many cases, the decision that the child was to be adopted was made early in the pregnancy. This meant that the mother carried a child, expecting that the child would not remain with her after the birth. The impact of the separation, therefore, was already being felt by the mother before the child was even born.

In his book, *Grief Counselling and Grief Therapy*, Worden describes studies undertaken in cases of terminal illness, where family members and friends have been advised that there would be no recovery. Worden describes how those who are expecting to become bereaved often experience what is known as *anticipatory grief* (Worden, 1991, pp108-111). These studies have explored whether or not having the opportunity to anticipate the bereavement assists in achieving the tasks of mourning.

It was observed that even though anticipation could be expected to help mourners to accept the reality of the event, sometimes they still denied it. It was found that anticipation did not help mourners to work through the pain resulting from the loss, as it seemed to cause an increase rather than a decrease in their anxiety levels. It was also noted that mourners often prepared themselves for the expected loss, by rehearsing the changes in relationships and in their own behaviour, which they expected would occur after the death. This often puzzled others, who did not understand what was happening.

These observations are very relevant to the situation of mothers who were expecting, prior to the births of their children, that a separation and therefore a loss was going to occur. Many mothers report that, although they knew that there was very little hope of their being able to raise their children, they still refused to acknowledge this and lived throughout the pregnancy with a fantasy that there would be a last-minute reprieve. Some report high levels of anxiety throughout the pregnancy, which were actually exacerbated, not relieved, by the expectation of the separation. Many mothers have said that they tried to distance themselves emotionally from what was occurring, in order to prepare themselves for their loss. Those close to them often misunderstood and misinterpreted their efforts to rehearse the changed relationship which they would have with their child, after the birth and anticipated separation. Worden's observations of anticipatory grief among those expecting to be bereaved fit very well, therefore, with the grief experienced by mothers who were expecting to be separated from their children after their birth.

It is possible that a foetus can be affected by the emotions and experiences of the mother during the pregnancy. If this is the case, then babies born to mothers who were expecting to be separated from them may have absorbed some of the mother's anxiety and her rehearsal of the expected change in their relationship after the birth. If the mother was trying, during her pregnancy, to create an emotional distance between herself and her child, in order to prepare herself for the forthcoming separation, this may have adversely affected the child's sense of safety and security.

Separation

In *Adoption and Loss – The Hidden Grief*, I focussed on the separation experienced by family members when an adoption takes place, the losses involved in such separations and the grief which results from those losses. I described the concept of *disenfranchised grief* and how this applies to adoption separation. Grief is disenfranchised when it results from a loss which is not openly acknowledged, publicly mourned or socially supported. Most societies recognise the needs of those grieving a bereavement and rituals, such as funerals, are designed to support those who are mourning a death. There are other losses in our lives, however, which are not so commonly acknowledged in our communities and for which no accepted rituals have been created.

Adoption separation is one of those losses. A mother and child are united prior to birth. After the birth they become two individuals, but those two individuals then constitute a family unit, which may also include the father of the child. The family breakdown caused by adoption creates a situation of loss. If that loss is not recognised, however, there will be no understanding of the appropriateness of grieving that loss. People do not generally associate loss with adoption, but, in fact, adoption is firmly grounded in loss. In my experience, all of those whose children are adopted by others have experienced this separation with a degree of anguish. For those who are adopted, no amount of caring and concern can erase the knowledge that, for whatever reason, they have been raised apart from the families into which they were born.

When a child is adopted, the parents lose their child and the child loses two families. Not only the parents, but also other family members, such as grandparents, may feel the loss of that child to the family. Because adoption has for so long been promoted as a positive outcome, there has traditionally been no support for those who grieve an adoption separation. For parents and children who are separated by adoption, however, there is a suffering that comes from living with the physical and emotional distance created by the adoption. Because of the separation, both parents and their children exist in a life situation, from which a very important person is missing. No amount of occupational success or material comfort can compensate for that missing relationship.

Parents who were separated from a child through adoption often buried their pain and hurt for many years, in part because of their confusion over whether or not they had made a decision of which they could be proud. They were usually told that, by agreeing to the adoption, they were making a wise choice for their child. This suggested to them that mourning the separation would be selfish. Many of those parents, however, after the adoption had taken place, began to feel a deep sense of shame at having allowed themselves to part with their children. Because of this shame, they often chose not to reveal the details of their experience. Because of the secrecy surrounding their loss, they were not in a position to grieve publicly.

In many cases, grieving the loss was impeded for the mother by those who thought that they were making the experience easier for her. Because of the social stigma attached to out-of-wedlock pregnancies, hospital staff sometimes erased the details of the birth from the mother's record, in order to protect her from exposure. Medical personnel even pretended, in some cases, that mothers were not in hospital to give birth, but had undergone a surgical procedure. This denial, although often well-meant, was actually counter-productive, as it prevented the mother and others from confronting reality.

For the children who were removed from their families to be adopted, their experience of the separation and the loss was quite different. Although many believe that babies taken from their mothers do exhibit signs of mourning and are aware on an emotional level of what has occurred, for adopted people, an intellectual understanding of the implications of that separation does not occur until they are much older. In many adoptive families, there has been no recognition of the losses experienced by the adopted children and so there has traditionally been no support for the grieving needs of adopted people. They also may have been made to feel that mourning the losses created by their adoption separation would be selfish, as they may have been encouraged to believe that being adopted was to their advantage.

For many adopted people there is a sense of unreality about the fact that they existed prior to being adopted. It is sometimes difficult for them to comprehend that they had an original name and identity and that they were a member of two families, prior to becoming a member of their adoptive family. Some adopted people are not even aware that they have a birth certificate which verifies that original identity and, in some places, it is impossible for adopted people to access those birth certificates. Many more, however, are now able to establish the difference between who they are (ie their actual identity) and what they are called (ie the name on their legal birth certificate).

Although adoption is based on loss, adoption separation rarely involves either rejection or abandonment. If an adopted person feels that they were rejected or abandoned by being adopted, then it would be helpful to them to test those feelings against the reality for their parents at the time. Genuine abandonment of babies is very rare. In fact, if parents had had any idea that their children were going to have those feelings, then they would have had more reason to resist the idea of adoption. Many of them did not resist, because they were told that by allowing their children to be adopted, far from abandoning or rejecting them, they were actually doing them a great favour and showing how much they cared about their well-being.

While grieving following a death generally assists the bereaved to come to terms with their loss, the lack of opportunity to grieve an adoption separation has serious on-going consequences for those who have been separated from family members by adoption.

Chapter 2
Adoption Grief

What are the outcomes of not going through the grieving process following an adoption separation?

Grief

In one sense, every adoption is a tragedy, as it means that a child has been separated from his or her parents and families. However, because adoption has for so long been presented as a positive event, this has added to the confusion and guilt which have made productive grieving so difficult, for parents as well as for adopted people. The grief of family members separated by adoption is disenfranchised and therefore is often not experienced at the time of separation, the way it would be if the loss were of a more conventional type. It is interesting, therefore, to explore how those involved in adoption separations handle their grief after the adoption has taken place.

Grieving is a very personal matter and each person's response to a loss will depend on many factors, in cases of adoption separation as well as in cases of bereavement. It needs to be acknowledged that people grieve in different ways. Some people do not recognise their own behaviour as grieving, because, while some grieve with tears, others do not. Worden states that, '…for some, grief is a very intense experience, whereas for others it is rather mild' (Worden, 1991, p31). Worden says that for some, grieving lasts a short time and for others a long time. He also states that personality structure can be a factor in response to loss, as can the degree of support provided by family and friends. While acknowledging that such variations exist, I believe that some general guidelines can be useful.

Grief is not only the *expected* response to a loss, it is also a *positive and beneficial* response, because grieving allows us to process our loss. We expect those who have lost a loved one through death to grieve that loss and community support is generally provided for that grief. Because of the lack of community understanding of the grief which follows adoption loss, however, there has been an unfortunate lack of community support for adoption-related grief. The secrecy and denial involved in adoption have contributed to the difficulties in resolving adoption-related grief. For too long those seeking help have been made to feel inadequate and have been labelled as having made a 'poor adjustment' to their situation. In fact, they are the fortunate ones who are approaching the issue with openness and honesty and are already on the path to healing because of their awareness.

Mothers who were separated from children through adoption were not given permission to grieve at the time of their loss. It is not surprising then that so many of them come to feel that they have never quite regained their equilibrium. I believe that this explains why mothers often report that their sadness and anger actually increased after the adoption took place. Taking into account everything that we know about grief, that is to be expected. They have been denied every opportunity to perform grief work because their grief has been disenfranchised by society.

After the Vietnam War, American servicemen who talked about how they had suffered, talked about having been 'sent to make murder in the name of virtue'. They were drawing attention to the fact that they were not expected to suffer because they had 'done the right thing' by fighting a supposedly just war and representing their country in an honourable fashion. The pain that they suffered as a result of their war experiences was often discounted, therefore, because of the nature of their role. Parents who were separated from children through adoption have felt similar feelings, as they were asked to surrender their newborn babies in the name of virtue. Their pain was also often discounted because they had supposedly acted in their children's best interests.

Over the years, the grief related to the adoption loss has an impact on the lives of those involved, although its effects are sometimes subtle and often not recognised as being related to grief. Mothers often try to process their adoption loss experience in a variety of ways. Some mothers return at some stage to locations related to the conception or birth of their child, in the same way that victims and perpetrators often return to the scene of the crime. Some mothers work very hard at holding on to whatever memories they have of the birth, because afterwards any chance to create memories with their child was taken from them. They hold on, therefore, to the little that they have. Other mothers do not even have any conscious memory of childbirth with which to console themselves.

Most parents who were separated from a child through adoption did not boast of the event. In fact, they often kept it a secret for many years. Usually an event is kept secret because of shame. If those involved had been proud of the adoption, they would have wanted to discuss it openly. It is also interesting to consider how consenting to adoption changed from being an unselfish, generous act, which was how it was portrayed before the event, to being one of which to be ashamed, which is how it was often perceived after the event. Many who grew up adopted also did not draw attention to that fact. They often had mixed feelings about being adopted, as it was difficult for them to comprehend how and why it had happened.

Generally speaking, I believe that parents who have been separated from children through adoption are not fully able to comprehend what they have lost, until their child reaches adulthood. While the child is still a minor, parents often go into a self-protective mode, as they are too fragile emotionally to confront their loss at that time. During this period the only way many parents can cope with the situation is to put their child to one side emotionally on a temporary basis and wait. While their children are still minors, many parents try to persuade themselves that adoption has been best for their children and have difficulty considering any other possibilities, until the child becomes an adult and they are forced to confront the reality. During this period, parents often feel the need to justify the separation from their children in terms of the children's best interests, in order to subdue the rising panic which they feel, as their children progress towards adulthood without them. Because of this, I believe that, when research is being conducted, it is appropriate for the views of parents whose children are still legally minors to be considered separately from the views of parents of adult adopted people.

Mothers who have been separated from a child through adoption sometimes have difficulty in their relationship with their next born child. Perhaps they resent this child for not being the lost child. Perhaps having a child and being able to nurture the child forces them to confront the reality of what the loss of the other child means. It may be that they are so emotionally distracted by thoughts of their lost child, that they are unable to devote the necessary emotional energy to building a relationship with this subsequent child. Perhaps their pain is too vivid and they are not able to be emotionally available enough to that child. They may be afraid of loving that child too much and are fearful that somehow they will also lose that child and so they maintain a degree of emotional detachment in order to protect themselves. Some mothers, however, become overprotective towards their subsequent children and are inclined to smother them emotionally. Sometimes the child who follows the lost child exhibits psychological disturbances, to a greater or lesser extent, such as obsessive-compulsive disorder or depression.

One of the principal tasks of grieving is adjusting to the environment from which the lost person is missing. In the case of an adoption loss, this usually means living as if the lost person no longer exists, while inwardly living with the awareness that, to the best of one's knowledge, the lost person actually does still exist, but is no longer a participating member of one's social system. Parents and adopted people often find themselves leading what feels like a *double life*. They carry a secret knowledge which they feel is socially unacceptable and they live with the fear of discovery. This fear causes a very real strain and can result in physical and emotional manifestations. In this way they carry their grief with them and learn to live with it covertly. Adopted people were often raised with a sense of gratitude and loyalty and a wish to ensure that their adopters felt confident and secure in the belief that they had acted in their children's best interests. Because of this, they tended to suppress and deny any feelings of loss which they experienced as a result of the separation from their families of origin.

Losses are also particularly keenly felt on dates such as anniversaries of particular events (conception, birth, signing of adoption consent, adoption being finalised) and family gatherings (Christmas, Mother's Day, Father's Day, birthdays). Many people have been able to anticipate and mark these events in a meaningful way. Those affected may create the opportunity to set aside a time in the day which involves acknowledging the loss created by the adoption separation. Time can also be scheduled for self-nurturing, spending time with those who are able to be supportive, or focussing on the opportunities for growth provided by the adoption experience. Others may wish to create a ritual to mark the date, such as planting a flower or writing a letter. These times can provide opportunities to work through anger and develop ways to use that anger productively, in order that it does not turn into bitterness and the desire to hurt.

In many cases grief has been misdiagnosed as depression. If a woman attended her doctor, for example and said that her husband had just died and that she was very sad, it is unlikely that the doctor would prescribe anti-depressant medication, as her sadness would be the expected response to her loss. Many women have attended medical personnel because they were grieving the loss of their children through adoption, however, only to have their grief misdiagnosed and to be encouraged to use medication. The grief of adopted children and adults is often also misdiagnosed, as many health professionals do not recognise the impact of the adoption separation on those who are adopted.

The impact of disenfranchised grief

Those who have been affected by adoption separation experience the same outcomes as other people whose grief is disenfranchised. Their suppressed grief can manifest itself in physical as well as emotional disorders. They may become depressed, develop emotional disturbances and sometimes physical illnesses. For some, the outcome is that they become high achievers and may suffer from anorexia or obsession with body image. However, for others the outcome is that they suffer from low self-esteem and may find themselves in abusive relationships. Sometimes they withdraw from society or succumb to substance abuse. Sometimes they have difficulty forming healthy relationships.

Their grieving often becomes chronic. They usually have difficulty dealing with subsequent losses, because they did not learn how to grieve productively, in what, for most of them, was the first major loss in their lives and so they simply do not know how to do it. When they experience other losses in their lives, they tend to repeat the pattern of behaviour that they learned at the time of the adoption separation and suppress their grief again.

Mourners whose grief is disenfranchised are cut off from social supports and so have few opportunities to express and resolve their grief. The result can be that they feel alienated from their community. The lack of recognition of their grief often results in them holding on to it more tenaciously than they might otherwise have done. Grieving an adoption loss is also complicated by issues of guilt and shame.

Sometimes, however, those who have been separated from family members by adoption are described as having made a 'good adjustment' to their situation and are said to be 'coping well'. What this often means is simply that they learn how to seek approval and to suppress their true feelings.

The outcomes of having suppressed the grief resulting from an adoption loss are many and varied. It would be impossible to list comprehensively the variety of ways in which the grief suppression can manifest itself. Often it is only later in life, with hindsight, that those affected can comprehend their behaviour in terms of grief reactions. Worden notes that those who are not comfortable with expressing their feelings openly can respond to loss with 'various types of acting-out behaviour which serve as grief equivalents' (Worden, 1991, p118).

One area of life in which the impact of this grief suppression is often manifested is in the realm of personal relationships. For some, they feel that they do not want to repeat the experience of separation and loss and so they choose to protect themselves by not forming close relationships. Others form relationships with people who are dependent and therefore less likely to leave them. Others make sure that they end relationships before the other party has the opportunity to do so.

Anger is a common component of grieving. Worden notes that if the anger following a loss is not expressed, '...it may be retroflected – turned inward and experienced as depression, guilt, or lowered self-esteem. In extreme cases, retroflected anger may result in suicidal behaviour, either in thought or in action' (Worden, 1991, p43). Many who have not experienced the grief resulting from their adoption separation have found themselves, over a period of years, exhibiting signs of depression.

In her book *The Anatomy of Bereavement*, Raphael writes about living with loss and describes what happens when a child is separated from his mother. When the mother returns, the child is comforted. If the mother never returns, however, the child can develop 'a painful vulnerability'. The child is always hoping for the return of the mother, but moves into self-protection mode in the meantime without her. The child may learn from this experience not to express emotion. Raphael states that when grief is repressed in this way, it can block the ability to empathise. This can lead to numbing of emotions (Raphael, 1983, p402). This may be the reason that some parents perceive the adult children they lost to adoption as being self-absorbed and unsympathetic.

For some who suffer an adoption loss, they bury the grief from their adoption separation and the outcome is that their reactions to other events are suppressed also, as they fear allowing their emotions to surface. It may appear to others, therefore, that these people are cold and lack emotional responses. In fact, they are, perhaps subconsciously, holding in all deep feelings, to avoid triggering an emotional reaction, which they fear would overwhelm them. For these people, when their grief finally is allowed to surface, they can find themselves recalling many emotional events along the way, to which their reactions at the time seemed muted.

For others, any loss event triggers the grief which they felt at the time of the adoption loss and they react in what appears to be an extreme manner to what may be considered by others to be minor losses. These people have no tolerance at all for loss and appear devastated at events, which others would take in their stride. In the case of adopted adults, this behaviour is sometimes incomprehensible to those around them, as there has often been no recognition that the adoption, for them, was a loss experience. Parents' behaviour also may appear bizarre, either because those around them have no knowledge of the loss of the child, or because they do not understand it as a loss experience.

People act in the way that they do because of the meaning which they ascribe to the circumstances of their life. They think, for example, that it is better for them to deny the facts and put the truth to the back of their minds because it feels more comfortable that way and so they act accordingly. When that way of manipulating events no longer 'works' for them, they must seek another. Eventually, hopefully, they will come to understand that the way to grow and learn from their adoption experience is truly to experience it, to grieve their adoption loss and to proceed through grief towards healing.

Mourning

According to Worden, grief is the personal experience of loss, while mourning is the process through which people go (Worden, 1991). Worden feels that the mourning process can be seen in terms of phases. Although those who have experienced adoption separation are generally unable to perform public grieving, it seems that they often do, perhaps without realising it, pass through these phases of mourning.

While Worden was referring to mourning following a bereavement, I have found his work to be very relevant to the mourning which follows an adoption separation. For example, he suggests that, 'There is a sense in which mourning can be finished, when people regain an interest in life, feel more hopeful, experience gratification again and adapt to new roles. There is also a sense in which mourning is never finished' (Worden, 1991, p19). It is important to be aware that the aim of mourning is not to lead the bereaved back to the position which they occupied before their loss occurred. Worden is very clear that trying to achieve this would suggest a failure to perform the tasks of mourning (Worden, 1991, p18).

The first phase of mourning, as outlined by Worden, is usually *numbness*, when people have difficulty accepting what has happened. The second is *yearning*, when people become angry and want the event to be undone. The third phase is *disorganisation and despair*, when mourners find it difficult to function and the fourth is what Worden calls *reorganised behaviour* when the mourner is beginning to regain equilibrium.

Mothers who have experienced an adoption separation frequently report a sense of numbness in the period immediately following the separation. A lack of response in babies who have been removed from their mothers to be adopted has often been observed also. This could be evidence of the children's experience of this numbness.

Many mothers also report much anger and wishing that the event (ie the separation) could be undone. Mothers frequently say that all they wanted was to have their baby back with them again. For adopted people, this anger frequently presents in acting-out behaviour and opposition throughout childhood and adolescence, although they rarely would be aware of the reasons behind their behaviour.

The phase of disorganisation and despair, for both parents and children, may cover the period during which the adopted child grows up. During this phase, each party is living without the other, trying to make sense of their situation and wondering if the future will hold any sort of resolution for them.

For many parents, the loss of their child to adoption has been a closely guarded secret. Even for those who have shared the information with people close to them, it is not a subject which is generally discussed frequently. In most cases, the feelings associated with the loss remain unexpressed and unexplored, at least until the lost child becomes an adult. Sometimes, sadly, those feelings are never explored or expressed.

I have formed the view that this burial of feelings while the child grows up is, in fact, a protective measure undertaken in many cases subconsciously. I believe that living with the grief on a day-to-day basis and being unable to resolve it can create a constant state of anxiety and can place an enormous emotional strain on parents. I have known parents who had contact with their children after the adoption had taken place and before the children reached adulthood. In some cases those parents were living in what appeared to be a chronic state of depression.

I believe it to be, in fact, a constant state of unresolved grief, which is not buried but present in their everyday existence. In some cases, quite understandably, this creates an intolerable situation. Sadly, if those parents terminate the contact because it is so painful for them, they are sometimes castigated as being uncaring and selfish. They are often blamed for having disappointed their child, by not fulfilling the terms of the original agreement. What they are doing, in fact, is protecting themselves from a situation which places an unbearable strain on their emotional resources. We will not know for many years what the long term effects of such contact is on the adopted children.

Finally, there comes a time when those affected seek to reach the final phase, that of *reorganised behaviour.* According to Worden, this is the expected final stage of the mourning process. However, because of the particular nature of the loss resulting from adoption separation, this phase is often delayed and may occur at any time in the lives of those affected. The urge to enter this phase, for both adopted people and their parents, often comes when the adopted child reaches adulthood, although they may not act on this urge immediately.

Once the commitment has been made to take action to move into the phase of *reorganised behaviour*, those affected may actually re-experience the initial phases of mourning. After making a decision to address adoption loss issues, a sense of numbness is common and those involved are initially unable to see their way forward. This may be followed by a reduction in the sense of numbness, as a deeper understanding dawns of how the separation, which occurred before the adoption took place, has resulted in losses for both parties.

This realisation may then cause significant feelings of anger and resentment to arise again. Those feelings may lead to a temporary sense of powerlessness and a lack of direction. Eventually, however, there comes the desire to achieve a sense of emotional wellness.

I believe that this is the missing piece of information, which solves the mystery of why those who have been separated from a family member by adoption seek to achieve a personal recovery, by exploring the significance of their adoption experience. They have a subconscious desire to move through the phases of mourning in relation to the loss created by the adoption separation and to reach a state of 'reorganised behaviour'. Because personal recovery work is a part of the adoption grieving process, it can give rise to intense emotional reactions.

Chapter 3
Personal recovery

How can the experience of adoption separation be integrated into people's lives?

Personal recovery work

Personal recovery can be very valuable for both adopted adults and their parents. It is a way of freeing up the energy that has been tied up in suppressing their grief. After a degree of personal recovery has been achieved, that energy can then be used to move forward with healing. If personal recovery work is not undertaken, then those affected by adoption separation can remain locked into denial and the anxiety which results from it.

One of the reasons for undertaking personal recovery work is to learn to live with the loss. Although the losses caused by adoption separation have been painful, it is not productive for those involved to persist in having an unhealthy attachment to their pain. We can learn to celebrate our survival instead of apologising for it.

Because family members separated by adoption were told, either overtly or covertly, that their feelings of loss and grief resulting from the separation were not valid, they have often lost trust in their own emotions. I believe that we are all born with a sense of self-preservation which assists us, if it is supported and allowed to develop, to make choices and judgments which are in our best interests. Because their judgment was challenged at the time of adoption separation, many of those affected lost trust in that ability to care for themselves. I believe that there is a link to the inner self which is seriously damaged by the inappropriateness of the adoption separation and that, from that time on, many struggle to reconnect with that protective inner voice. The result is that, after an adoption separation, many have made choices which were not in their best interests.

I have come to believe, however, that that damaged connection can be repaired. I have witnessed that repair happen many times. If we return to the experience of separation and feel the sense of loss, express the grief and know that those emotions are valid and appropriate, then we experience a sense of healing. This can allow us to renew our acquaintance with that innate sense of judgment. We can, in fact, rewrite the script which we learned from others, who told us that our feelings were inappropriate. We are then better able to make choices which will genuinely be in our best interests, because we will be allowing ourselves to experience authentic emotions.

Personal recovery work can be undertaken at any time after the adoption separation, but parents generally find that their feelings mature as their children mature. Anecdotal evidence suggests that, for parents, a change in attitude to their adoption experience often takes place when their adopted children reach adulthood. This can mean that even if a degree of personal recovery work has been undertaken while the child is still a minor, it can be helpful to revisit that work once the child becomes an adult. Adopted people may have grown up in families where their issues of loss and grief were recognised and acknowledged. However, they too will benefit from taking responsibility for their own personal recovery work and addressing those issues when they reach adulthood.

The aim of personal recovery work is to explore the experience of adoption separation, to understand it and acknowledge it and to validate your feelings about it. Personal recovery takes place on two levels. On an intellectual level, you are aiming to understand what happened and on an emotional level, you are aiming to get in touch with how you feel about what happened. I believe that for those separated from a family member by adoption, their feelings of sadness and grief are actually the expected outcome of having experienced a loss which has often been unacknowledged or misunderstood. Acknowledging the loss can be the first step towards enjoying a more contented and productive life.

Many parents are deterred from acknowledging the loss of their child by feelings of guilt and shame. These can be reduced by exploring the historical and social context of the circumstances which led to the adoption. Many adopted adults are deterred from acknowledging the loss of their families by community attitudes, which encourage them to express gratitude for having been adopted. They can learn to see their adoption in a more honest light, by confronting the reality of what it has meant for them to be separated from their families.

It is helpful for those affected by adoption separation to understand that they are entitled to grieve. I believe that their grief will always be with them and that it is up to them to choose how to address that fact. If they try to repress and deny their grief, it may force its way into their lives, in ways that can be uncomfortable and distressing. I believe that this is often what has happened when a 'nervous breakdown' has been said to have occurred. If they do not take an active part in addressing their grief, there is also the danger that it will engulf them and prevent them from enjoying a productive life. This situation has sometimes been diagnosed as chronic depression. Both of these outcomes are disempowering and undesirable.

If you have been separated from a family member by adoption, it is important for you to recognise that your grief can be managed and incorporated into your life. The feeling of anger and the sense of loss associated with this grief will vary in intensity at different times in your life. The notion of *grief resolution* has different meanings for different people and, for me, it is not a useful goal, as it implies that some people may succeed, while others may fail. I believe that it may be much more productive for family members separated by adoption to be supported to respect their experience and acknowledge it as a permanent, but manageable, part of their life. Many people talk about the personal recovery process as a kind of 'thawing out' which allows the grief to come to the surface and be experienced.

Undertaking personal adoption recovery work will make you feel better about yourself. It will help you to understand the events of your past better and to change how you think about what has happened in your life. Although you cannot change what has already happened, you can achieve a sense of control in the present and make choices for the future. Adoption recovery work is designed to be empowering, to remind you that every child born into the world is a great gift and to help you to be able to celebrate that fact. Our adoption experience also helps us to have compassion for the tribulations of others and to put life's other challenges into perspective.

Adoption separation creates a loss which is difficult to grieve. When you decide that the time has come to address that grief, this personal recovery process can be undertaken alone, with a close friend or family member or with professional support. The recovery process can be supported by attendance at an appropriate support group and by reading about the experiences of others. Some people like to talk through their history and others prefer to write it. I originally recounted my story in counselling sessions and then some years later I wrote it in *Adoption and Loss – The Hidden Grief*.

Undertaking a process of personal recovery is a positive, productive act, which shows that you are aware of the need to attend to your adoption issues in order to move forward. Taking this step is a sign of emotional strength. Telling your story will lead to healing and understanding, to renewed courage and increased generosity of spirit. If adoption has left us with only bitterness and sorrow, we have failed to grasp the opportunities which life has offered us through our adoption experiences.

Re-grief therapy

The process of re-grief therapy involves reworking, at a later time, a bereavement which had not been satisfactorily resolved. It has two goals; to understand why mourning was not completed in the past (operating at an intellectual level) and to help those affected to experience their grieving emotions in the present (operating at an emotional level). During the course of re-grief therapy people's 'frozen emotions are stimulated and reawakened'. As with regular grief therapy, the outcome of re-grief therapy is an increase in self-esteem and a decrease in guilt, as well as an increase in positive feelings about the lost person (Raphael, 1983, pp385-6).

I have chosen to apply re-grief therapy to reworking an adoption loss. In the case of adoption loss, I believe that, in order to understand the reasons why the mourning was not completed, it is important to understand first of all how and why the loss occurred. An informed exploration of the circumstances leading to the separation often results in the griever having more positive feelings about their adoption experience.

Exploring these issues can be instrumental in bringing the pain and grief to the surface and it can then be experienced. Pain is not necessarily a negative outcome and preventing people from experiencing pain is not always in their best interests. Pain is not always avoidable and it is sometimes necessary in order to produce something new. Childbirth, for example, is rarely accomplished without pain.

Once we understand the basis of our pain, we are in a better position to treat it. Patients would not feel confidence in a doctor, for example, who wrote a prescription for pain relief medication rather than first of all seeking the cause of the pain. Pain is a message that there is an area that needs attention. Experiencing the pain created by adoption separation can, in fact, be a way of creating a renewed sense of self.

Anger is a common response to a loss and it frequently occurs with regard to adoption loss. Many people are angry that an adoption took place, but this does not necessarily mean that they are angry with any particular person. Re-grief therapy may cause suppressed anger to come to the surface. Anger can be destructive if it results in vindictiveness and cruel accusations. Anger can, however, be a productive and helpful emotion when it is understood and managed. It may be appropriate to talk to those involved in the adoption about one's anger so that there is openness and honesty in those relationships. Telling someone about your anger is very different from expressing your anger towards that person.

This section, in which I outline a proposed programme of personal recovery, is addressed to mothers. Much of the work which I am suggesting, however, applies also to fathers. A similar programme of personal recovery work could be devised, based on this one, for adopted adults. For them, personal recovery is about exploring honestly, without guilt or shame, what it has meant to them to grow up in an adoptive situation. This will include attitudes in the community towards adoptive families as well as the adopted person's emotional response to knowing that they were adopted and how this changed over the years. This programme, based on Raphael's model of re-grief therapy, can be adapted to suit individual needs.

Understanding how and why the adoption loss occurred

a) where to begin

Because adoption separation is a profound experience and because the emotions attached to it have often been buried for many years, re-grief therapy can itself be an emotionally traumatic process. It is wise therefore, to prepare oneself for such an undertaking and to remember that no matter how difficult it may seem, this process can lead to a personal recovery from the trauma of adoption separation. It takes courage to begin this process but the rewards can be great.

In the endeavour to recover, the telling of your story has enormous therapeutic value, as it can unlock your grief in order that it can be experienced. There are several ways you can choose to tell your story. You may wish to write it, to share it with a close friend or family member, to discuss it with a professional counsellor, to share it in a group setting or to meditate on it alone. You may tell your story in one way first of all and then later in another. Whichever method you choose, if it involves an audience, then it is wise to make sure that your audience will be accepting and non-judgmental.

Telling your story involves exploring, examining and considering exactly what happened, how it happened, why it happened and how you felt when it happened. It involves looking at what happened long before the adoption event and also at what happened long after the event. Hopefully, as you move through the events and emotions which surrounded the loss of your child, you will begin to see connections between those events and emotions. Eventually a clearer picture will emerge for you of exactly how and why it all came about. When you decide to tell your story, make sure that you choose to do so in a manner which gives you a sense of control. Pace yourself and move at a rate which suits you. If you can, set aside time to tell your story - a time in your life, a time in your day. Be prepared for the intrusion of life's crises but do not be distracted from your goal. Try to choose a time for your story when life will not be placing too many other demands on you. Telling your story will itself be demanding and will use up much of your physical and emotional energy.

Eventually you may choose to share your story with a wider circle of associates. If your experience has been a secret one for many years, sharing it will be a major event in your healing. It takes a lot of energy to keep a secret. Once you free yourself from that secrecy, you will then have energy to spare and you can use that energy to nurture the relationships which have been affected by the secrecy. Adoption has, for many people, been associated with shame, secrecy and deceit. Releasing yourself from those negative constraints will bring with it an enormous sense of relief. Freedom from secrecy is always beneficial and it is never too late in your life to achieve that. Think of what you are doing if you choose to live in a situation of deceit. By deceiving others, you are not 'protecting' them, you are actually disempowering them and retarding their growth and development. It is never too late to learn that lesson and to give another person the gift of being able to confront the truth.

The purpose of this exploration is not to apportion blame, not to justify or make excuses, nor is it to decide whether actions were right or wrong. Its purpose is to assist you to make links and connections between your life events and the values, beliefs and motives that give them meaning. For many mothers telling their story in this way is the first time that certain patterns have become obvious and this often leads to empowering moments of clarity and acceptance and to a reduction in feelings of guilt and shame. Considering that many mothers have spent many years feeling guilty and ashamed about having become pregnant, about having allowed their babies to be adopted and also about the fact that they were still suffering from their loss, this is a huge achievement.

b) keep in mind

Deciding to tell your story takes courage, even before you make the choice to share it with others. You may be afraid of revisiting the pain which you experienced at the time of the separation. Remember that pain is sometimes useful. Avoiding pain can be restrictive and harmful to your development.

When you recall events in your life which were hurtful, rather than seeking someone to blame, you can gain from those experiences by focussing on what you have learned from them. If, on the other hand, you focus on yourself as having been a victim, you may be blocking your own personal development.

Many mothers find it difficult to move beyond their sense of shame and guilt. Rather than focussing on your feelings of guilt, focus on your motives and intentions. You may have had certain views of the events of the past and certain feelings about them, but some feelings are not helpful or productive. You cannot change events which have already happened in your life, but you can change how you think about those events and that can lead to changes in how you feel about them.

Be prepared for intense feelings to come to the surface while you tell your story. Acknowledge them and accept them. They are yours and they are legitimate. Feel them and own them. You may even experience dreams or flashbacks. Events and conversations, which you had buried, may come to the surface. Bear in mind that you will be very vulnerable during this time and be careful to protect yourself.

If you can, try to factor in activities such as outdoor walks while you tell your story. You will gain in many ways. You will expend the energy that might arise as a result of tapping into some hidden anger. You will be able to relax and recover from the distress of reliving traumatic events. You will also be in touch with the natural world and be renewed and energised by that.

Activity can be a sign of grieving. Sometimes when grief comes to the surface, people want to be very busy. Be ready for this to happen. With adoption grief this sometimes takes the form of talking and writing about adoption or even counselling others.

c) social history

Attitudes to illegitimacy have changed markedly over the last century. While there have always been some professional people (social workers, doctors, religious leaders), who have understood the value of a child being raised within the family of origin, those who did not share this value have argued for mothers and their children to be separated. Often there were other factors which seemed to be more important than family unity.

In some situations which resulted in adoption, the pregnancy was planned, but before the birth occurred the circumstances changed. More often the pregnancy was unplanned. When the pregnancy was confirmed, the mother then had to consider her options. For some, marriage made the pregnancy more socially acceptable. The remainder found themselves giving birth as single women. For some of those, the father of the child not only promised support but also fulfilled his promise. For others the parents of the mother provided the support. For the remainder, adoption was almost always the result.

Some mothers did not tell their families that they had given birth. Perhaps they thought that the love of their family was conditional on them conforming to expected social behaviour and that they would not be accepted when it became obvious that they had not conformed. It seems that, in some situations, family members were not valued for who they were, but for how they behaved. Perhaps some children were valued more highly than others in such families, depending on the circumstances in which they were conceived.

I believe that in every case of adoption (I am referring here to those which took place with legal consent, not those which occur in some countries without consent of the parents) of which I have been made aware, the decision was made by someone, most often the mother and sometimes also the father of the child, who believed that the child would have greater opportunities for a productive and fulfilling life in an adoptive home.

Sometimes the decision was not made by either of the parents of the child, but by their parents or by authority figures such as doctors, ministers of religion or social workers. Of course, this belief in the overall benefit to the child of being adopted was just that – a belief. No one could have known whether or not this would be the outcome of the adoption decision. Determining where the responsibility lay is not the same as looking for someone to blame.

It is my view that, generally speaking, mothers who were separated from their children through adoption were not raised in families in which children were valued for their own sakes, or in which it was clear that being with one's own family had some intrinsic value for the child. Perhaps reputation and standing in the community were more important. Perhaps the mother herself felt that the child would have been better off in another family. In that case, this may mean that she herself had not felt accepted and valued in the family in which she grew up.

Perhaps the mother found herself alone and at the mercy of professionals, who took advantage of her vulnerability and managed the adoption regardless of her feelings. In these cases, it is interesting to consider why those mothers were alone and vulnerable. If they had grown up in a family in which they and their child were valued, they may not have found themselves in that position. They would have had a family member, or perhaps the father of the child, with them, to prevent their exploitation.

There were certainly some women who had no family and who found themselves alone and pregnant. They may have chosen as the fathers of their children men who did not value them. Perhaps this was because they did not sufficiently value themselves. There are also significant numbers of adopted women who lose their own children to adoption. Some have not learned the value of a child in a family because they did not grow up in their own family. Because adopted people have not had genealogical continuity in their own lives, they may be unable to comprehend its significance for their children.

d) growing up

It is useful to remember that, as we grow up, we absorb the values and belief systems in which we are raised, although, later in life, there usually comes a point in our lives at which we are experienced enough to challenge them. During adolescence, however, the value system of the family in which we are raised has an enormous impact on our own priorities and decision-making. So too do the values and standards of our peer group. We must also consider the beliefs and traditions of the cultural or social group to which our families belonged, as well as the bigger picture of the historical events and movements which were occurring at the time in question.

It is helpful to explore the history of our own parents, the values with which they were raised and the historical period in which their own belief systems developed. In some families, religion has been a directing force. In some families war and immigration have been factors. It is interesting to explore the growth of the relationship between our parents. How did they meet? Did their parents approve of the relationship? Were they in some way pressured into marriage? Some mothers have discovered that their own parents married because of an unplanned pregnancy. If this resulted in an unhappy marriage which was the subject of regret, then those parents may have had fears for their children finding themselves in a similar situation. Those parents, therefore, may not have pressured their children into a hasty marriage, if an unplanned pregnancy occurred.

In many social groups only two choices were presented by parents to their children who were facing an out-of-wedlock pregnancy – marriage or adoption. If the parents had their own reasons not to promote a hasty marriage, this family may have been supportive of adoption, believing it to be the lesser of two evils. In some social and cultural groups, however, children were valued for their own sake and it would have been unthinkable for a child to be raised outside of the family. In those cases, adoption would not have been presented as an appropriate outcome and support would have been provided for the child to be raised within the family group.

Explore your childhood and your childhood experiences. It is important for you to understand the meaning of those experiences for you and how you felt as a child. Consider issues such as communication, or lack of it, in your family, your feelings of self-worth, approval-seeking behaviour, religious and cultural influences, the relationship between your parents, relationships with siblings, gender issues, your sense of security and safety as a child, family expectations and priorities. Think about any major changes and losses which occurred in your childhood. Perhaps there were changes in the family members; deaths, divorces, people moving away. Perhaps there were changes of environment; new homes, new schools, new countries.

Then think about your adolescent years, how the changes of puberty were approached in your family, moral standards and expectations during the era in which you were a teenager, your role models and your first romantic experiences. Again, the emphasis is on how you experienced this period in your life and the impact that it had on your sense of your own value. Consider whether or not you feel that you had a need for approval at this period in your life, whose approval was important to you and why this might have been.

Next, consider the relationship between you and the person who became the father of the child who was lost to adoption. Some mothers were raped, some were taken advantage of by older partners, some had become what was viewed at the time as promiscuous, perhaps as a result of previous sexual abuse and some were involved in loving relationships. Think about the extent to which you understood the connection between sexual relationships and pregnancy, the use of contraception and how awareness of the pregnancy occurred. Try to recall how news of the pregnancy was disclosed and what the immediate outcomes of that disclosure were.

e) pregnancy and childbirth

While you describe the experience of being pregnant and the events that surrounded the pregnancy, think about issues of control and power and consider whether you felt a sense of disempowerment during this time. Think about motives and beliefs as well as expectations and priorities. It was often during this period that plans for the future were made. These plans were often made by others and your views and feelings may not have been considered. Consider when the adoption decision was made and whose interests it was expected to serve. When considering the adoption decision, mothers often see themselves as both victim and perpetrator - neither perception is helpful.

Description of the birth itself can be traumatic for many mothers, especially for those who have never been invited to describe it before. Many mothers are unable to describe the experience of giving birth, however, either because they were not conscious during the event or because they have since lost the memory of it. For many mothers the outcome of the trauma experienced at that time has been loss of memory. For some there are moments which are clear and others which are completely lost to them.

It is often difficult for mothers to recall events which occurred shortly after the birth of their child. Most report a feeling of numbness and a sense of emotional distance from what was happening. Some can recall nothing for some time after the birth. Many mothers recall the behaviour and attitudes of medical personnel and other professionals, however, including issues around whether or not they were able to see or hold their babies.

Accessing relevant documents can be an important element of personal recovery work for mothers. Receiving a copy of your child's birth certificate, for example, validates your experience and your relationship to your child. Hospital and social work records may also be useful. Any other documents relevant to the adoption, which can be obtained, may assist in the exploration of the events. It is wise to bear in mind, however, that obtaining those documents can itself be a challenging experience and may resurrect a range of buried emotions. It may be wise to have a support person with you when accessing such documents.

Be aware also that the loss of your child may have been complicated by other, related losses. Many women lost the relationship which they had shared with the father of their child. For some, they had to leave employment or study or even move to a different area. Many lost friendships and close relationships within their families. For most mothers the adoption had an irreversible impact on their relationships with their parents. Reliving the loss of your child may bring to the surface connected losses which have also not been adequately grieved.

f) what has happened since

By not raising the children which they had created, parents were actually encouraged to avoid taking responsibility for their actions. They were told that the right thing to do was not to accept the logical consequences of their behaviour. It is interesting to consider how they may have internalised that and the impact which that may have had on their behaviour later in life. It seems that some parents learned that not taking responsibility was acceptable behaviour and therefore acquired the habit of blaming others. On the other hand, some felt that they had shirked their responsibility and took it upon themselves thereafter to be very responsible. They sometimes blamed themselves, throughout their lives, for anything that did not turn out well. This may have created a degree of tension in people's lives, which can have an impact on their general health.

Many parents are afraid to succeed in their lives as it may appear to others that they had gained from not raising their children. This puts them in a no-win situation. If they do well in life, then they feel guilty. If they do not succeed in life, however, that allows others to suppose that their child was indeed better off without them. Many parents also feel that they have no right to be happy - how could you be happy when you lost your child? Often this means that they become resentful and angry when people tell them that they seem to be 'doing well'.

Part of the recovery process is sorting out the difference between facts and beliefs. It was a fact that the woman was pregnant. It was a belief held by some that she could not provide the best care for her child. It was a fact that she had had some kind of sexual relationship which had resulted in the pregnancy. It was a belief held by some that she was by virtue of that an immoral person and an unfit mother. While some facts are indisputable, beliefs can be challenged and they change over time. We each give our own meanings to the events of our lives.

Part of the recovery process is making links and connections and being able finally to understand what has been happening in one's life. For example, a mother might have found that throughout her life she has had an aversion to signing her name and that completing forms of any kind is difficult for her. When it is pointed out to her that the first time she signed her name, as an adult, on a 'form' was to sign an adoption consent for her child, then her aversion is explained.

Some mothers have great difficulty remembering dates. When they realise that they had blocked out the date of the birth of their lost child, then they understand that having 'forgotten' that very important date, they would have felt guilty allowing themselves to remember dates which related to much more trivial events.

Mothers who have been separated from children through adoption often go to great lengths to ensure that subsequent children have a strong sense of their identity and history. I wrote a life history for each of the four children I raised and researched my ancestors for several generations back. This gave my children a sense of belonging and being connected.

Some mothers have had great difficulty enjoying Mother's Day celebrations prior to reuniting with their child. They have, in many cases, sabotaged the attempts of the family to create an enjoyable day. When they realise that their guilt would not allow them to accept themselves as worthy of praise in their mothering role, then it becomes clear to them why they covertly made sure that they did not enjoy that day. Once they understand their own actions, they can make an effort to change their behaviour.

It is useful to explore the on-going impact that the loss of the child has had on your life. For many mothers, secrecy has been a major factor in their lives since the birth of their child and this has had a noticeable impact on their relationships with other people and on how they view themselves. Some became involved in another relationship shortly after the loss of their child. Some experienced another pregnancy soon after. Some had no further children.

It is also helpful to examine the impact of the loss of the child on how you have dealt with subsequent significant events, especially losses. In many cases, where a significant loss had not been appropriately grieved, there was a very intense reaction to subsequent losses. In other cases, there appeared to be little reaction to subsequent losses as a behaviour pattern of shutting down emotionally had been established at the time of the loss of the child. Once you have a deeper understanding of your past, think about the strengths and strategies which you have already displayed, in order to be able to live with your experience and consider how you can put those strengths to use during the remainder of your life.

g) summary

The aim of personal recovery work is to mourn the losses created by the adoption. Although it may not be possible for parents or adopted adults to declare that issues have been addressed and will never recur, nevertheless it is possible to identify signs that mourners have been able to assimilate their loss. Worden suggests that one sign that mourning is nearing completion is when we reach a stage in which times without pain can be enjoyed (Worden, 1991, p18). The pain may return but, over time, it erupts less frequently and less intensely. Personal recovery work on adoption separation issues can bring both parents and adopted adults to a point where they are able to enjoy life without feeling guilty.

When you have a sense that you have achieved a level of acceptance of the issues surrounding your adoption separation experience, it is likely that you will feel more comfortable sharing your experience with others. This can serve the dual purpose of giving you a sense of ownership of your experience and also contributing to community education and awareness. If you are able to present your experience to others in a powerful and confident manner, then you will find that you no longer feel the sense of shame that you may have felt prior to undertaking personal recovery work.

For many, seeking reunion is a natural progression from the acknowledgement and exploration of the impact of adoption in their lives, which occurred during their personal recovery work. Those who have already achieved a degree of personal recovery prior to reunion bring more clarity and awareness, as well as less anger and sadness, to the reunion experience. For those who have not already acknowledged their grief, the experience of reunion itself can provide the impetus to embark on a programme of personal recovery work. Whether or not a reunion takes place, however, personal recovery work plays a vital role in the journey towards healing for those who have experienced an adoption separation.

Part II
Interpersonal Recovery

Chapter 1
Adoption Reunion

Why do some seek reunion while others try to avoid it?

Understanding the purpose of reunion

There is, sadly, a lack of understanding in the community of the reasons behind the efforts of those who have been separated from family members through adoption to achieve reunion. It is my belief that the wish to reunite is part of the awareness, although often subconscious, of the fact that there exists a grief which has not been addressed. I believe that those who attempt to create a reunion experience have a deep-seated desire for emotional wholeness, which leads them in that direction and that reunion plays a major role in the process of mourning the adoption losses.

It is my view, from hearing of and reading about many adoption reunion experiences, that those who desire reunion are seeking to find a way to experience the grieving process, which they were denied at the time of the original separation. I believe that desiring reunion is a positive sign, as it is a striving for openness, growth and healing.

Because they are not consciously seeking grief, however, many people are shocked and dismayed when the reunion leads to painful grieving experiences. It is important to be aware that *the reunion does not create the grief.* The grief is caused by the initial separation, although that grief is often not experienced until the reunion takes place. I believe that seeking to bring about a reunion is a positive step towards resolving the grief resulting from the separation. For this reason, I believe that it is appropriate for reunion between family members separated by adoption to be encouraged and promoted.

There is also, however, a loss which is experienced when reunion occurs. Reunion represents the loss of ignorance and fear. Reunion can replace ignorance with knowledge and fear with confidence. While learning the truth may create a temporary situation of unrest, it is also a great opportunity for growth. At the time of reunion, adopted people often mourn the loss of the self that might have been, while parents often mourn the loss of the child that they could have raised.

Those who seek reunion rarely have a clear understanding of their hopes and expectations. I believe that it is unhelpful and unrealistic to expect people to be able to articulate why they desire to make contact. Those seeking reunion are, in my view, showing a wholesome desire for addressing their grief and promoting healing. Many say that they did not have a clear understanding of why they were seeking reunion until after it occurred and that the reunion produced outcomes which they could never have predicted. For many, it is only after the reunion occurs that connections between certain events in their lives are made.

I believe that wishing to be reunited with family members is a natural response to having been separated from them. I do not believe that seeking out a family member from whom one has been separated by adoption is an activity that requires explanation and justification. It could be construed that asking family members to explain and justify their attempts to contact each other can be a way of giving them the subtle message that such behaviour is unacceptable and somehow suspect.

Those who seek reunion are showing a desire to address the grief tasks that they have been unable to work through immediately after the separation. One of the principal issues in the unresolved grief which follows adoption separation, is the lack of finality of the loss. With a death, there is eventually no option to the mourners but to accept that the deceased is unavailable. With an adoption separation, there is always the possibility of a reunion. This possibility is one of the factors which inhibits the grieving process and often means that the grief remains unresolved.

I believe that many of those who have experienced an adoption separation are seeking a form of grief resolution. One way to try to achieve this is to create a situation which represents this finality, which has been missing from the adoption separation experience. I believe that this desire for finality and therefore for a full grieving experience, leads many people to seek a reunion. The reunion is in some ways a mirror image of the original separation. Reunion represents the closing of the circle of separation which began at the time of the adoption.

The reunion is able to take the place of the finality which we associate with death and which is missing from adoption separation situations. The reunion is the death of hopes and fears, the death of wondering and imagining and the beginning of facing reality. For many, although their grief has been present since the original separation, it has been to a large extent unexpressed and perhaps even unacknowledged. Some have been able to express their grief prior to reunion and to have it acknowledged and validated. For them the reunion allows them to proceed further down the path of grief resolution. For many people, however, their grieving begins at the moment of reunion, when they are confronted with the reality and the finality of their loss.

The relationship between mother and child is central to adoption. A mother and child constitute a family. I have attempted in this book to chart the journey from the *disintegration* of a family due to adoption, to the *reintegration* of the lost family members into each other's lives. The two people most closely connected prior to the adoption are the mother and the child. When reunion is being considered, therefore, the two principal parties must be the mother and the adult adopted child, although, hopefully, other members of the family, including the father, siblings and grandparents, will also wish to be actively involved.

Many mothers have 'buried' their lost children

emotionally and then 'resurrected' them when the time was appropriate. These mothers know deep inside that if they ever meet their children again, that those children will be unrecognisable compared with how they looked when their mothers last saw them (if, indeed, they did see their children) and so they have to be prepared, in a sense, for a new 'incarnation' of their child.

What happens when the child is an adult is that it is as if they have been lost and then re-found. This is similar to the tradition in some societies of having a public burial after a death, followed by the welcoming of the deceased back, as one of the ancestors. In this way the deceased takes on a new and very clear role. This could be viewed as being a healthier way of dealing with death than emotionally 'holding on' to the deceased in their former role and therefore having difficulty accepting that, in that role, they are gone forever.

For some parents, it is difficult for them to merge the two facets of their child's identity – the baby and the adult. Mothers have been known to bring gifts to their adult child at the time of reunion, which would be appropriate to a young child, such as blankets and soft toys. These are also gifts which have a comforting function. Many mothers have a strong desire at the time of reunion to hold and touch their children. The adult child may not feel comfortable with such behaviour, however and it would be wise for mothers to be cautious and to take their lead from their children.

Interpersonal recovery, like personal recovery, has both an intellectual element (replacing ignorance with knowledge) and an emotional element (replacing fear with confidence). The intellectual element involves the exchange of information. Parents are able to inform their adopted adult children of the circumstances which led to their adoption and adopted adults are able to inform their parents of the events which have occurred in their lives since the adoption. Adopted adults may have previously been given erroneous information. Parents seldom have received any information at all. The meeting itself, as well as the exchange of information, may bring many emotions to the surface.

Why some people refuse reunion

It is unwise to make any assumptions in a potential reunion situation. The person who makes the first contact has no way of knowing how far the other party has gone in processing and experiencing their grief. Even being the one who makes the contact does not necessarily mean that you are at an appropriate stage in your healing to accommodate the reunion well. It is always important to remember that you do not have the power to change the other person and that, in some respects, you will have to accept them as they are. Although a reunion by definition involves two parties, it may only have been sought by one party. In such cases, the invitation from one party to be part of a reunion is often an invitation to the other party to begin acknowledging their loss and experiencing their grief.

All of those who know that they have been separated from a family member by adoption choose whether or not to prepare themselves for the possibility of reunion. In some ways the situation is similar to facing the deaths of our parents. We all know that there is a strong likelihood that we will experience the deaths of our parents. This means that we cannot honestly say, when this occurs, that it was totally unexpected. Some of us are more prepared for these events than others, however. All of us will no doubt experience the deaths of our parents with some degree of shock and anguish, but we cannot genuinely claim, when the time comes, that we 'never thought this would happen'.

Many people have put the possibility of adoption reunion to the backs of their minds and chosen not to prepare themselves for that possibility. They cannot genuinely claim, however, if it does occur, that it has taken them totally by surprise.

Some people do not respond well to an invitation to be

part of a reunion, because they are at a place in their life where they feel it necessary to concentrate on their own needs. They may not be willing to introduce the reunion factor into their current situation. They may feel that all of their energies are being used already and that they do not have the inner resources to confront the reunion issue. For them, it may be a question of postponing a reunion until what seems like a more appropriate time.

Sometimes mothers refuse to accept adult adopted children into their lives because they cannot love themselves and own up to the truth. They have been damaged by the adoption and feel guilty and ashamed, not of the child but of themselves. Sometimes adopted adults refuse to accept their parents into their lives because they feel more comfortable minimising the impact of adoption on their lives and do not wish to make themselves vulnerable by exploring it. In situations such as these, those affected are not 'rejecting' the other party but rather are choosing not to proceed with their healing at that time. This is where some personal recovery work could be very valuable.

People sometimes say that they choose not to seek out a lost family member, because of fear of 'disruption'. They fear either the disruption to their own life or causing disruption to the life of the other party. In fact, our lives are made up of 'disruptions' – falling in love, having a child, taking a holiday, moving house, starting a new job. Many of these 'disruptions' are viewed in a positive light and, indeed, are considered to be expected elements of adult life. The sort of disruption you may cause, if you contact a family member from whom you have been separated by adoption, is that you can offer them the opportunity to address issues which have been buried and have perhaps been causing them stress and anxiety. This is actually a 'disruption' which has the potential to have a very positive outcome.

Many people fear a reunion because it is a step into the unknown; it is a step from which there is no stepping back. They fear that this event will change their life forever. People often fear grief and it can take courage to make a deliberate decision to confront one's grief. When people make statements like *I couldn't cope with it* or *I'm not interested*, often what they mean is, that they fear the impact of the grief and they know that dealing with it will be difficult and so they are choosing to avoid confronting it. If reunion is delayed, it is often a sign of the degree of damage which has been caused by the adoption separation and the fact that there is a great deal of healing to be done. There are many instances where one party is unprepared for reunion and their grieving and healing begin only after contact has been made.

The word 'interfere' also crops up frequently in discussion about adoption reunions. Interference occurs in adoptions because a child is adopted only after there has been interference with the initial bond between mother and child. It is that original interference which creates the need for recovery, of which reunion is such a large part. Suggesting that someone become involved in a reunion is not interfering; it is inviting. It is part of adulthood to consider invitations and either to accept or refuse them. Being invited to take part in an event is not generally viewed as interference.

Some people refuse to agree to be involved in a reunion because they claim to be concerned about the impact on others. In trying to take on responsibility for the feelings of others, however, they are, in fact, often using this as an excuse for their own fear. Some of those affected by adoption separation lost the ability to trust their own feelings, when they were told that their feelings of grief resulting from the separation were inappropriate. They then find it difficult to deal with the option of contact.

Some adopted people refuse contact with their parents as a way of expressing their anger with them. They refuse to respond to invitations as a way of punishing the parents and exercising control over the situation. Sometimes they claim to be protecting their adopters. Parents sometimes refuse contact out of fear, or out of anger with the whole experience. They also sometimes claim to be protecting others such as their other children or their partner. Often, rather than protecting others, such behaviour denies them the opportunity to grow, to learn and show generosity.

What can happen after the reunion?

Many reunions result in on-going, close relationships. Some result in on-going troubled relationships. In some cases, the relationship continues for some time and is then terminated. Even if the relationship is a strong one, it still needs to be nurtured. If the relationship is troubled, steps can to taken to improve it. If contact has broken down, action can be taken to restore the relationship.

Many have wondered why, in some reunion situations, contact continues for some time and then ceases. This can happen because, after reunion has taken place, some people want to go back. It often happens when a death occurs, that a survivor might wish that things could go back to the way they were before, when they were able to spend time with the lost one and look forward to a future with them. They wish that the death had never happened, as life was pleasanter before.

For some who experience an adoption reunion, they also would like to go back to the way life was before it happened. Life may have seemed simpler then and more comfortable and so they cut off from the other party, as if they had never met and try to get back to the comfortable place which they had inhabited, before they confronted the reality that reunion provides. It is not possible, of course, to undo a reunion experience, any more than it is possible to reverse a bereavement experience. *Trying to move back, by definition, prevents people from moving forward.*

Happily, there are many families in which close, strong bonds are formed after reunion and these enrich and enhance the lives of all the family members involved.

Chapter 2
Reunion Grief

How can reunion outcomes be explained in terms of loss and grief?

Why does reunion produce grief reactions?

I believe that the initial separation caused by the adoption creates a loss which results in a grief reaction. For many people this grief reaction is buried because they do not receive community support and understanding for their need to grieve. For some, there comes a time in their lives when they acknowledge this series of events and allow themselves to experience this grief. Sometimes this is done as a deliberate strategy, when someone decides to undertake personal recovery work, by exploring and acknowledging the impact of adoption separation on their lives. If personal recovery work has not been undertaken prior to reunion, however, the grief may spontaneously come to the surface, without any planning or preparation on the part of the person involved. This can be alarming and unexpected.

The reactions to contact from a family member of those who have been unaware of any buried grief are very revealing. Throughout our lives it is not uncommon to be contacted by people who are strangers to us. This occurs for a variety of reasons, but rarely causes severe distress of any kind. It is rare for deep emotions to result from a contact by a person who is unknown to us. Contact from family members from whom we have been separated by adoption, on the other hand, often results in extreme emotional reactions. Responses which are common to such situations are anger, joy, sadness, relief and sometimes a lack of reaction which could be described as numbness.

These responses often occur in situations where those contacted claim not to have been aware of the impact of adoption on their lives, prior to the contact. It seems to me highly unlikely that contact from a person who is, in a sense, unknown, could, in itself, *create* such deep and dramatic emotional responses. It makes much more sense to me to accept that the contact actually *awakens* emotions which have been buried and have therefore been, until that moment, unacknowledged.

Many, who had previously claimed not to have suffered from the impact of adoption, find that the contact itself allows feelings, which they were not aware that they had, to come to the surface. I believe that it will help those involved to understand their reactions, if they work on the premise that the reunion does not create feelings of grief; in fact it allows already existing feelings to be exposed and experienced. This is a positive, productive step in the process of coming to terms with one's adoption experience and assimilating it into one's life. Releasing that buried grief allows people to move forward and grow in self-knowledge.

I believe that the move towards personal recovery is an attempt to facilitate the grief associated with a major loss event. In many cases, it is successful to some degree. The reunion itself is a major recovery event and is therefore an important part of the process of healing. If the grief, which has been dormant since the separation, has already been addressed through personal recovery work, then the reunion may feel more manageable and the impact of the reunion event may be less marked. If, however, no attempt at personal recovery has been made before the reunion event takes place, then the impact often appears to be greater, as the grief has been dormant for a longer period of time and has not already been processed, even in part. In situations such as these, grief may have become chronic. I believe that this is why many reunion experiences resemble bereavement situations and can cause grieving behaviour to be exhibited.

When the original loss occurred (ie the separation caused by adoption), neither party was able to perform the tasks of mourning. Those people who later seek reunion have, albeit sometimes subconsciously, recognised that they are suffering from delayed or chronic grief and are attempting to give themselves the opportunity to work through those grieving tasks. What then seems to happen is, that when the reunion occurs, this event echoes the original loss event, by highlighting the lost opportunity to spend those intervening years together. This may precipitate grieving, as if the loss had just occurred. Reunion becomes, in that way, a trigger for the grieving that was not able to take place at the time of the initial loss. This explains why reunion so often results in emotions which are similar to those which follow a bereavement ie sadness, numbness, a sense of unreality, anger, guilt and fear.

Unfortunately, few people are aware of the nature of reunion grief and there is an expectation in the community that the reunion will be an event to be enjoyed and celebrated. This has caused many people to feel confused and guilty about their grieving. It becomes difficult, therefore, for those involved to find a way to express the grief which arises. I believe that when there is a wider understanding of the reasons why reunions result in grief reactions, then those who are experiencing a reunion will be able to receive more support and acceptance, both from those close to them and from professionals working with them.

Anticipatory grief at the time of reunion

With regard to anticipatory grief, Raphael indicates that those who are anticipating a bereavement go through phases of denial, angry protest and acceptance (Raphael, 1983, pp50-53). Many fluctuate between phases and the degree of acceptance varies from time to time. People tend to hold on to what is familiar and resent the impending change. One emotion may be prominent. It could be anger, sadness, regret, resentment or guilt (Raphael, 1983, p396).

The first response to news that death is inevitable is usually shock, numbness, disbelief, denial as well as a sense of unreality. This shock must be absorbed. Raphael believes that the way that the news is broken is important. It can be done in an 'assaultive' way, leaving the person traumatised and distressed by the experience, as well as by the news. Once the acceptance has set in, then come fear, anxiety, helplessness, angry protest and resentment. Denial may reappear at any time. This can force people to confront past guilt and they may withdraw from the world into themselves. It often causes people to review their lives. Raphael says that with a forthcoming bereavement, the signs of anticipatory grief are sadness, fear, anger, distress, guilt, sorrow, despair and depression. When the death occurs, the principal sensation is often relief. Regardless of the anticipation, however, the actual death will trigger grieving.

These emotions also occur in those who have been in contact with a lost family member and for whom a reunion is a possibility. Anticipating a reunion is in many ways similar to anticipating a death. At the time of contact, before the reunion has occurred, many exhibit denial. There are also many angry protests. Often these phases are followed by acceptance. It is impossible to determine how long each of these phases may last. I have known people to remain in denial, sometimes combined with angry protest, for many years. These are the people who refuse to continue contact. Hopefully they will eventually move on to the acceptance phase.

In some cases, the other party wearies of waiting for this to happen and precipitates a reunion (eg by arriving at the other person's home unannounced) to force the family member involved to enter the acceptance phase. As with anticipating a bereavement, some appear to have reached acceptance, only to slip back sometimes into one of the other phases. Some people are resistant to change and choose to avoid acceptance for as long as they are able.

As with the first response to the fact that a death is inevitable, the first response to contact from a family member is often shock, followed by numbness, disbelief and denial. It can take time for the initial shock to be absorbed. As with news of an impending death, it is important how the news of reunion contact is broken. In some cases, very tactless and insensitive approaches have caused people to stay for longer in the shock phase than would be considered comfortable. Once the person has absorbed the shock and reached a level of acceptance of the situation, then fear is often the predominant emotion. Fear of a possible change in relationship can cause people to hold on to feelings of helplessness and resentment. As with anticipation of a death, denial can recur at any time and can be used as a 'comfort zone' to avoid confronting the reality of the impact of the contact. As with a death, regardless of the anticipation, the actual reunion triggers grieving.

Normal grief reactions

Worden describes characteristics of normal grief following a bereavement (Worden, 1991, p22). These reactions and emotions are also common in adoption reunion circumstances. Sometimes those involved are puzzled by their behaviour and their emotions as they have no clear understanding of why they occur. They are, in fact, components of normal grieving behaviour and when people understand that reunion creates the atmosphere for the grieving of the adoption separation to occur, they see that their reactions are grieving reactions and, as such, are exactly what one would expect to occur.

The characteristics outlined by Worden are: bodily distress (many of those who experience an adoption reunion find themselves frequently tearful and anxious or suffering from insomnia, indigestion and other physical features suggesting anguish), preoccupation with the deceased (many describe thinking about the reunion frequently and for some people the relationship has some of the elements of a love affair), guilt (reunion often causes feelings of guilt to surface for parents when they are confronted with the reality of the separation of the child from the family, while some adopted adults also feel guilty that they seem to have been the cause of so much distress to their parents), hostility (hostility is a very common feature of adoption reunions and sometimes takes the form of refusal of contact) and inability to function as one had before the loss (for many people the reunion experience seems to 'take over' their lives for a period of time and they sometimes describe their reaction to the reunion as verging on 'obsessive').

Worden also lists other feelings which are manifestations of normal grief, which are also common in adoption reunions (Worden, 1991, p22) – sadness (when reunion occurs, many people feel an overwhelming sense of sadness but cannot explain exactly why they are so sad), loneliness (many who are experiencing reunion feel isolated and have a sense that no one else understands and often find that support groups can be very helpful, as can reading of the experiences of others), fatigue (the reunion experience can be very emotionally draining and this can lead to physical exhaustion, which may result in an appearance of apathy or listlessness), helplessness (the reunion experience can be so overwhelming that some people just feel unable to cope and become very dependent and needy), shock (no matter how well prepared people think they are for the reunion event, the reality of it often results in a sense of shock), yearning (many people find that they do not want to be parted from the other party once a reunion has occurred and they 'can't get enough' of that person's company, sometimes feeling that they want to try to make up for the time apart by spending as much time together as possible), numbness (after a bereavement, or an adoption reunion, many people experience an emotional numbness, which can be an automatic protection mechanism against feelings which may seem overwhelming).

Finally, anger is considered to be a manifestation of normal grief. Confronting the reality of the adoption separation frequently engenders feelings of anger. Worden talks about the child who became separated from his mother in the shopping centre. He experienced fear and anxiety, but when she returned to him, rather than expressing love and relief, the child displayed anger and 'kicked her in the shins'. Worden says that this is the child's way of saying, *Don't leave me again!*

Adopted people often express anger towards their parents when they are reunited with them, or when they are offered the opportunity to reunite. This reaction is similar to that described by Worden of the child separated from his mother. When the reunion occurs, or when reunion is offered, the adopted adult is reminded that they were 'left' by the parents as an infant and their anger at this separation comes to the surface. This anger causes some adopted adults to refuse reunion.

With parents, the anger is often displaced or directed towards some other person, often blaming them for the adoption. The line of reasoning is that if someone can be blamed, then they are responsible and hence the loss could have been prevented (Worden, 1991, p23). Some people direct anger against themselves and become depressed or even suicidal.

It is important to remember that these are all normal components of grieving experiences and that their intensity reduces with time. When someone dies, for example, others would consider it normal for us to be tearful for a considerable period of time, depending on how intimate our relationship was with the deceased. It is also considered normal for a bereaved person to be preoccupied with the deceased for some time. When we realise that adoption reunion precipitates a grieving experience, then it becomes clear that this behaviour is also 'normal' in reunion circumstances. If the grieving takes its expected course, the intensity of all of these grieving characteristics will fall to a manageable level over time, as it does following a death.

Complicated grief and adoption reunion

According to Worden, if mourning is not undertaken, grief can become 'complicated' (Worden, 1991, pp71-77). Worden describes complicated grief reactions under four headings: chronic grief reactions, delayed grief reactions, exaggerated grief reactions and masked grief reactions. Adopted people and their parents may exhibit signs of all four complicated grief reactions.

A chronic grief reaction is one that is excessive in duration ie it lasts for an unexpectedly long time after the loss has occurred. Some adopted people seem to carry a deep sadness into adulthood. This may be because they are still grieving the loss of their parents. Some parents also seem to carry a deep sadness for many years after the adoptions of their children. They may still be grieving the loss of those children. This long term sadness results from those involved having been unable to perform any of the tasks of grieving at the time of separation. Overt sadness around holidays and anniversaries can also be a sign of a chronic grief situation.

A delayed grief reaction is one in which the emotional reaction experienced at the time of the loss has not been sufficient to the loss. This kind of grief reaction is also known as an inhibited, suppressed or postponed grief reaction. At some time in the future, the person may experience a reaction to a subsequent loss, which appears to be exaggerated and inappropriate. This is because the grieving from the original loss is being carried forward. This may occur because, at a time of loss, we instinctively feel that we wish to turn for comfort to 'an earlier attachment figure'. We are then reminded that this earlier attachment figure is missing from our lives and so we experience pain related to this earlier loss. Adopted people and their parents sometimes react excessively to subsequent losses in their lives, because they have not been able to process adequately the loss associated with the separation which occurred at the time of the adoption

An exaggerated grief reaction is one in which the person experiences the intensification of a normal grief reaction and feels overwhelmed by it. This can result in a type of grieving behaviour which is excessive and disabling and which can develop into psychiatric conditions, such as clinical depression and anxiety disorders. Some adopted babies are emotionally withdrawn and do not form attachments with their adoptive families. Their symptoms, had they been present in an adult, could have been classified as a depressive or anxiety disorder, including phobic behaviour. Substance abuse in adulthood is also a feature of this type of grief reaction. Some parents, in the period after the loss of their children, were classified as suffering from a depressive or anxiety disorder. Some were hospitalised as a result, without any recognition that their condition was actually a grief reaction.

A masked grief reaction is one in which people experience behaviour and symptoms which cause them difficulty, but they do not recognise that these are related to the loss which they have experienced. The symptoms which they develop are known as 'equivalents of grief'. Masked grief may be a self-protection mechanism, used to circumvent the grief process. The symptoms can be physical (unexplained pain or discomfort of some kind) or emotional (depression or acting-out behaviour). False euphoria after the loss event can also be a sign of a masked grief reaction.

Adopted people and their parents often show no outward symptoms of grief after the adoption separation takes place, but may suffer later in life from unexplained illness or sadness, which does not appear to relate to current events. This is often puzzling for those close to them. Some people mask their grief with intense activity. Such activity is common following bereavement. There are many whose lives have been affected by adoption separation, who expend intense energy on their careers. This may be a way of circumventing the grief process by keeping themselves so busy that they have no time to mourn.

Another consequence of complicated grief can be the avoidance of further close attachments in order to ensure that another grief experience does not occur, if relationships come to an end for any reason. This behaviour can be a consequence of adoption for both adopted adults and their parents. Some adopted adults appear to be emotionally detached and do not form long term relationships as adults, preferring to remain unattached. This kind of reaction has also prevented many parents who have been separated from children through adoption from having subsequent children.

How is reunion grief expressed?

Reunion grief can express itself in many forms, as does grief following a bereavement. Not everyone experiences the same intensity of pain or feels it in the same way. For some the main emotion is anger and this has not always been recognised as a grief reaction. Many have been puzzled by the degree of hostility expressed when family members have been offered the opportunity of contact. For those who do not understand that hostility is a common component of grief, some of the responses experienced can appear to be alarmingly extreme. However, when this hostility is viewed in a grief perspective, it becomes more comprehensible.

Anyone who has been present in a hospital ward, for example, where a death has occurred, may have witnessed much anger and hostility as the bereaved struggle to accept the reality of what has occurred. Often there is a search for someone to blame and a desire to make some sense of what has happened by making accusations. Similar behaviour occurs at the time of contact between family members separated by adoption. Anger and sadness come to the surface and there is sometimes a desire to blame and accuse. Bereavement often causes a deep sense of injustice and resentment. So too does adoption contact and reunion. In both cases, those affected are actually angry at the event (ie the death or the adoption) but they often direct their anger at the people involved. For parents, their sense of loss tends to increase dramatically at the time of reunion. With adopted people it seems more common that their anger increases suddenly at the time of reunion. When these feelings are understood and acknowledged, there is no need for them to prevent a relationship from developing.

Many parents and many adopted people are angry that the adoption took place and they may look for someone to blame. Parents sometimes blame each other, sometimes other family members or professionals; adopted people often direct their anger and outrage towards their parents. One of the commonest ways of expressing this hostility and sense of injustice is to refuse contact and reunion. This refusal is often an attempt to express a sense of injustice and resentment about the adoption, by punishing the other party for their connection with that event.

As with any grieving experience, a person who is experiencing an adoption reunion will not necessarily go through an identifiable series of stages of grieving in a clearly consecutive manner. Emotions will fluctuate. Sadly, expectations are raised and it is difficult to deal with what often appears to be regression. There may come a time when one party feels fairly comfortable in the relationship and has certain expectations of behaviour. The other party may then resort to either angry outbursts or long silences which often involve blaming, accusations and insults. While this kind of behaviour would always be distressing, it is often more difficult to accept if it occurs at a later stage in the relationship than it might have been earlier.

The reunion is in some ways a ritual event in itself and is often planned to some extent in the way that a funeral service is planned. The venue and the participants are selected, the date and time is set and personal preparations are made. In the same way that funerals do not occur without preparation, reunions are more likely to fulfil their purpose adequately, if some thought is given to where and when the reunion will take place and who will be present. Attempts to persuade those involved that a funeral or a reunion is a time for celebration have caused many people to feel confused and guilty about their grieving.

In some societies, public displays of grieving are not encouraged. This is evident in the 'stiff upper lip' mentality, where it is expected that mourners will repress their emotions, at least in public. In adoption reunion situations, many people also repress their emotions in public, by downplaying the importance of the event and their emotional reaction to it, in order to try to conceal their vulnerability. While it is not necessary for the grief to be expressed in company with the other party, it can be hurtful if one family member overtly minimises the importance of the meeting and the relationship.

As with grieving a bereavement, there are crucial points in time at which people can feel overwhelmed. In comparing reunion with bereavement, I consider the physical meeting to correspond with the physical death. Three months after the event is often a time when the grievers can go through a crisis. At this stage in the mourning process, the community generally withdraws the level of support which was provided immediately after the loss event, resulting in a feeling in the mourners of being unable to manage their experience. In adoption reunion situations this may be the time at which one party withdraws temporarily from the relationship, finding it overwhelming. An awareness that this is a common response in grieving behaviour can help those affected to be patient and understanding.

Anniversaries of the event are often challenging, especially the first anniversary. It is useful to mark the first anniversary of the reunion in some way which acknowledges its significance. Other challenging events are family occasions such as birthdays. While these are more significant in the first year, it is helpful for them to be acknowledged on an on-going basis as potentially painful events.

Reunion outcomes

Grief processing and the performance of mourning tasks have been described in various forms by many who have written about grief issues. In relation to processing the grief resulting from an adoption separation, I believe that the reunion experience can be very valuable. In my view there are four possible reunion outcomes in relation to grief processing.

There are those who experience reunion and, as a result of that experience, they are able to perform the mourning tasks and incorporate the adoption experience into their lives. There are others who experience reunion and resist performing the mourning tasks and so do not take the opportunity presented by reunion to address their issues of loss. For them the loss remains an on-going unresolved issue.

A third group desire a reunion but are unable to achieve it, because the other party remains unavailable to them. This can be as a result of death, refusal or simply the failure to locate the person sought. I believe that even when a physical reunion is not possible, a great deal can be achieved in the area of personal recovery. Confronting and acknowledging the impact of the loss in one's life and celebrating the positive aspects of one's experience can be useful, even if no reunion takes place.

Finally, there are those who refuse to make any effort to bring about a reunion. These people have, in my opinion, either not begun to perform the mourning tasks, or else their progress through these tasks has been arrested at some point, short of the logical conclusion ie seeking reunion.

Reunion and the Four Tasks of Mourning

In my first book *Adoption and Loss – The Hidden Grief*, I referred to the original edition of Worden's book, *Grief Counselling and Grief Therapy*, published in 1982. In this book I have referred to the revised edition, published in 1991. The tasks of grieving which Worden had outlined in the first edition of his book were altered slightly in the second edition and I have found the altered version to be more useful. Worden's tasks were created to apply principally to grief following a bereavement, but they are readily transferable to other types of losses.

With a bereavement, these tasks would naturally follow on from the death. In an adoption situation, however, it is difficult to achieve the tasks of grieving at the time of separation and it is my belief that the event of reunion creates the opportunity for those tasks to be completed. The decision to participate in a reunion is, in my view, a recognition of the importance of processing the grief in order to incorporate the adoption experience into one's life. Failure to process grief of any kind can have long term negative consequences. Worden describes the tasks of mourning as firstly, to accept the reality of the loss, secondly, to work through the pain of grief, thirdly, to adjust to an environment in which the deceased is missing and fourthly, to relocate the deceased emotionally and move on with life (Worden, 1991, pp10-18).

I explained in my first book why it is often impossible for family members separated by adoption to complete these tasks at the time of separation. For mothers, fathers and other family members, it is often impossible for them to accept the reality of the loss (task I), because they have no way of knowing what they have lost when the child is relocated away from the family. There is also often a sense of unreality about the events surrounding the birth and adoption, especially for those who do not directly participate. Adopted adults generally have no conscious memory of the separation from their families and so those events also have a sense of unreality for them.

Mothers and others involved were advised not to dwell on the loss of the child and there was no community support for them to work through the pain of their grief (task II). There was, in fact, no recognition that they had suffered a loss and so there was no expectation that they would have any need to grieve. Adopted adults were generally raised to believe that their adoption was an advantage to them and not a matter for grieving.

Because the child did not have the opportunity to become established as part of the original family, the loss that is involved is the loss of a potential family. As there is no way of knowing what that family would have become, it is impossible for parents to adjust to the family environment from which the adopted child has been removed (task III). Because adopted children have no way of knowing what their life might have been like had the adoption not taken place, they also are unable to adjust to the lost potential family environment.

Because the grief resulting from the separation was buried, those involved carried it with them. This prevented them from 'moving on with life' (task IV) with any sense of having emotionally relocated the missing family member(s). The missing family member, in fact, is usually still present in the consciousness, rather than being emotionally relocated.

I believe that those who seek reunion are attempting to create, through reunion, a situation in which they can experience these four tasks of mourning.

Task I – to accept the reality of the loss

When a reunion occurs there is a loss of fantasy, expectation and dreams. Reunion also confronts those involved with the reality of the relationship which could have developed, had it not been interrupted by the adoption separation.

For some, reunion also brings about the loss of the comfortable position which they had created, in which they consoled themselves by taking the stance that the adoption separation had produced positive outcomes and had not had a negative impact on their lives. Sometimes it is difficult for them to accept that this is not the case.

Some people have difficulty accepting the reality which has replaced their previous position. This reality may be welcome or it may not. Often people can hardly believe that the reunion has actually happened, especially if they have been anticipating it for a long time. It takes on an aura of unreality. Some people try to avoid acknowledging the reality of the reunion by minimising the significance of the event.

Accepting the reality of the loss is not only an intellectual task but also an emotional one. Anger can be a feature of this acceptance; anger at the other party, anger at oneself, anger at others. Adopted people might be angry at their parents for leaving them, angry at themselves for having enjoyed life regardless, angry at others for having colluded in it all. Parents may be angry with themselves for allowing the adoption to happen, angry with others who engineered it and even angry with their child who may seem indifferent to them.

Mourning will be facilitated if there is an intellectual acceptance of the actual relationship between the two parties and also an emotional acceptance, which involves comprehending the implications of it all. Rituals, such as obtaining written evidence of the adoption or creating evidence of the reunion, for example with letters or photographs, can help with this task.

Some people report vivid dreams during adoption reunions. Dreams can be the subconscious mind's way of validating the reality of the event. Reunion, ie physically seeing and interacting with the other party, allows those involved to experience the reality of the loss by allowing them to confront the real person, rather than the image which they have created in their thoughts.

Accepting the reality of the loss involves understanding that a family was created when that child was born and that that family was prevented from developing when the child was adopted. There is no way of knowing what kind of family would have evolved, but accepting that the adoption has created a loss experience for all family members is the first step in working through the resultant grief.

Task II – to work through the pain of the grief

The first task leads, apparently inevitably, to the second. When those involved begin to understand the enormity of the loss which they have experienced, the pain of the grief resulting from that loss will begin to be felt. If those involved in the reunion are not prepared for pain, then they may experience a feeling of fear and panic and wish to withdraw from the reunion experience. This is sometimes viewed by others as 'running away'. It may, in fact, be an attempt to avoid pain, which is caused by a lack of understanding of the source and the purpose of the pain.

Seeking to avoid the pain, therefore, interrupts the grieving process and leaves the griever in a kind of limbo, not knowing which direction to take emotionally. Experiencing the pain of grief is a natural response to reunion, as it is a vital part of the grieving process. Failure to work through the pain of the grief may result in physical symptoms or in aberrant behaviour. Any attempt to avoid the pain may prolong the grieving.

Generally there is no community support for reunion-based grieving as there is often the expectation that the reunion will be a joyful experience. Grief experienced at the time of reunion, as at the time of separation, is often disenfranchised, because the losses which are highlighted and created by reunion are not openly acknowledged, publicly mourned or socially supported.

Some people try to avoid the pain by shutting themselves down emotionally and refusing to allow the feelings to come to the surface. Some use alcohol or drugs to suppress the pain. Some people move away geographically to avoid confronting the pain. Some have euphoric responses to reunion, but these are often very fragile and short-lived. Sooner or later those who try to avoid grieving are forced to confront it. It is more comfortable and productive to acknowledge the need to grieve and allow it to take its natural course, rather than to try to avoid it and then be at its mercy.

Task III – to adjust to the changed environment

Adjusting to the changed environment will be easier to accomplish if the first two tasks of grieving have been fully experienced and not avoided. For parents, it is necessary for them to accept that the child whom they could have raised is now an adult and that their adult child has experienced a life which is entirely different from the one which might have been, had the adoption not taken place.

For the adopted person, it is necessary for them to accept that the parent who could have raised them has also experienced a life entirely different from the one which might have been, had the adoption not taken place. Both have had a life in which the impact of adoption has been crucial. The people they would have been, the relationships which would have grown and developed, are gone and can never be retrieved, just as if they had died.

An environment has been created by the adoption and that environment and its impact have to be accepted and the other, the lost opportunity, mourned, before progress can be made to the fourth task. It is impossible to predict how those involved will adjust to the new relationships which are created by the reunion experience, until it has happened. In the same way, it was impossible to know how parents would feel about the separation from their child until after the birth had occurred. The environment has changed post-reunion and a considerable adjustment is needed. As with a bereavement, three months after the event is often a crucial time. The initial intensity has worn off and community interest has waned. It can be helpful to focus at that time on what has been gained from the change.

It helps also to confront what the reunion means for one's own sense of self. If a poor adjustment is made, the reunion event, like a bereavement '…can lead to intense repression where the bereaved perceive of themselves as helpless, inadequate, incapable, childlike or personally bankrupt' (Worden, 1991, p15). Some people feel that it is impossible for them to make that adjustment and they try to escape from it. Some feel that they have temporarily lost direction in life, until they have been able to make the necessary adjustment. Others work against themselves by promoting their own helplessness or by withdrawing from the world. Most, however, eventually move forward. Those who do not manage to achieve this task can be '...held prisoner by a dilemma...[they]...cannot solve' in a 'state of suspended growth' (Worden, 1991, p16).

Task IV – to move on with life

Moving on with life requires acceptance of what has occurred and a focus on the positive aspects of the current relationships in order for a degree of peace and contentment to be given an opportunity to develop. If the three previous tasks have been fully experienced, there is hope that the moving on with life, which Worden proposes, can be successfully achieved. It is not reasonable to expect that the tasks of grieving will have been totally and finally experienced, however and there will always be times when the feelings undergone throughout the completion of those tasks will resurface. They can be experienced and accepted in the knowledge that they are a natural response to the reunion event and that they are manageable and will pass.

'Mourning ends when the mourner no longer has a need to reactivate the representation of the dead with exaggerated intensity in the course of daily living' (Worden, 1991, p16). In reunion, the task is to relocate the events of one's life and go forward with a sense of wholeness, without constantly regretting what might have been. Adopted people and their parents have had to shelve notions of their missing family members because of lack of knowledge. They can all come to understand that adoption is only one part of their lives. Not achieving this task would be trying to go back, to hold on to life as it was, as if the reunion had never happened. This could involve a return to secrecy and suppression of emotions and truth.

I believe that this is the missing piece of information, which solves the mystery of why those who have been separated from a family member through adoption seek to achieve interpersonal recovery through a reunion. They have a subconscious desire to complete the tasks of mourning in relation to the loss originally created by the adoption separation and to 'move on with life'. Because interpersonal recovery work is a part of the adoption grieving process, it can give rise to intense emotional reactions.

Chapter 3

Interpersonal Recovery

What issues may arise when an adoption reunion occurs?

Will it 'work out'?

Some people erroneously talk of reunions between family members who have been separated by adoption in terms of 'success' and 'failure'. I feel that this is an inappropriate and unhelpful way of looking at this complex situation. There are often family members, who have been part of the same family, who, as adults, choose not to spend time together. No one considers describing their relationships as having 'failed'. We simply accept that we cannot choose our relatives and that we do not always have much in common with them, nor enjoy spending time in their company. As adults we make those choices. Regardless of our choices, however, nothing changes the fact that we are related.

Unfortunately, some people expect the reunion, or the person with whom they are to be reunited, to do the recovery work for them. It is, in fact, the experience of reunion, not the person with whom you are reunited, which aids recovery. It is important to remember that we are each responsible for our own recovery, regardless of whether or not a reunion takes place or whether or not it meets our expectations. The family member with whom you are reunited is not responsible for providing you with what you need to recover. Everyone can achieve a degree of personal recovery regardless of their reunion opportunities. Your relative may or may not appreciate your needs and your experience. Regardless of how much or how little they have to offer, you can use the experience of reunion to aid your recovery.

It is helpful for anyone contemplating a reunion if they have made some effort to know and understand themselves, before attempting to get to know or understand the other person. Personal recovery work will help people to get to know themselves better. It can be a preparation for reunion but it can also be useful in its own right for those who never have a reunion.

If you are considering initiating a reunion, then it is wise to bear in mind that the person you are hoping to meet is an emotionally damaged person. The mother may have been damaged before the birth. That may be why this particular birth resulted in an adoption. She will certainly have been further damaged by the loss of her child and possibly also by a lifetime of shame and secrecy. The adopted person has been damaged by the loss of their families.

It is also wise to keep in mind that the other party may not have conducted any preparation for reunion and may need some time to come to terms with the reality of it.

The unknown factors

Each party to an adoption reunion is bringing with them certain unknown issues. Any or all of these can give rise to difficulties in the reunion.

Grief ~ You have no way of knowing to what extent the other party has recognised or experienced their grief. It is wise not to underestimate the depth of this grief, even though it may not be immediately apparent.

Experience ~ The other party may already have had experiences with family members, or even with partners or friends, which have resulted in apprehension or issues of trust. They may have been mistreated or they may have been indulged. On the basis of this, they may have certain expectations around the reunion.

Values ~ Values and beliefs are very important to how we view the world and our place in it. People's values vary widely and sometimes differences in religious or moral beliefs can cause conflict. Personal qualities valued by one person may be of no importance to another. This can lead to disappointment and anxiety. It is important to remember the need for acceptance and honesty in reunion relationships.

Knowledge ~ Some people take time and trouble to prepare themselves for reunion by reading, talking and reflecting. Others go into a reunion with absolutely no awareness of the issues which underlie adoption separation and reunion.

Emotions ~ Reunion is a very emotional time and some emotions may seem to be unreasonable or frightening. It can be useful to find an outlet for these emotions which will not damage the reunion relationship.

Personality ~ Even in families where there has been no adoption, children often have very different personalities from each other and from their parents. It takes time to familiarise yourself with someone's personal characteristics.

Intentions ~ Sadly, some people precipitate a reunion with the intention of punishing and may thereby cause pain. Others focus solely on what it is that they want from the reunion and show no concern for its impact on the other party.

Expectations ~ The parent and child may have been damaged by the separation and by the fact that they have been taught that their feelings around the adoption separation are not valid. They may both have learned not to trust and may have lost faith in their ability to respond appropriately to emotional issues in their lives. It is wise not to go into a reunion with unrealistic expectations.

Maternal Alienation

Forming a relationship with a family member from whom you have been separated by adoption is a unique experience. While it is for many people a joyful and fulfilling experience, it can also bring challenges and concerns. These are particularly evident in the relationships between mothers and their adult children. One of the reasons for the difficulties in such relationships is, I believe, the impact on the relationship of maternal alienation. The concept of maternal alienation grew out of studies (unrelated to adoption) in families where domestic violence and/or child sexual abuse had occurred. The description of maternal alienation which I have used is taken from an unpublished paper written in Adelaide, South Australia by Anne Morris in 1999.

a) as practised by fathers

The term *maternal alienation* is used in two ways. First of all it is used to describe a range of strategies used by some abusive men, deliberately designed to undermine and destroy the relationships between mothers and their children. The term is also used to describe the outcome of the use of those strategies, which can be a profound and long lasting estrangement between mothers and their children. Maternal alienation is considered to be a form of emotional abuse.

This undermining of the relationship between mothers and children renders the children very vulnerable, as they lose trust in their mother and in her ability to meet their needs. The children often form the view that their mothers were somehow responsible for the separation and they then blame them for the outcomes. Such children form a negative view of their mothers, which makes it difficult for them ever to form close bonds with them. In many cases, after these children have been estranged from their mothers, abusive fathers (or men acting in paternal roles) have been able to draw these vulnerable children into developing an unhealthy sense of loyalty to them.

b) as practised by the adoption system

It is my view that the practice of adoption has created its own form of maternal alienation, beginning with the separation of infant children from their mothers. In the same way that some abusive men have been able to alienate children from their mothers, I believe that the system of adoption has been able to alienate children from the mothers who have not raised them. Adoption has undermined and damaged the relationships between mothers and their children by separating them, by encouraging mothers to forget that they had given birth and by encouraging the children to regard another person as their mother.

The outcome of these strategies has been very similar in many cases to the outcome in domestic abuse situations where maternal alienation has been a factor. In many families where an adoption separation has occurred, the children have become vulnerable and have lost faith in their mothers. They may also have blamed them for the initial separation. Sadly, it is not uncommon to find that such children have formed a negative view of their mothers and so have found it difficult to form close bonds with them as adults. They may also, over the years, have developed an unhealthy sense of loyalty to those who did raise them. In this way a profound and long lasting estrangement between mothers and their children has been created.

Strategies used to achieve maternal alienation

a) by fathers

In order to create this alienation between mother and child, abusive fathers often denigrate the mother as a figure to be despised and elevate the father as both a victim and a hero. These tactics are usually even more successful if the mother is not physically present in the lives of the children and is therefore unable to present any contradictory picture. The mother in this way is isolated and punished.

Both the children and their mothers are being abused in these situations and the effects are often long lasting. This is especially true when there is no understanding of the reasons behind the estrangement. If an understanding can be gained as to how this alienation took place and the sort of manipulation which was involved, then steps can be taken to try to heal the rift and reverse the estrangement.

b) by the adoption system

Society has systematically denigrated the mothers of adopted children and accorded to the adopters the roles of heroes and saviours. Mothers were often hidden away physically at the time of the birth. They were not congratulated and honoured for their motherhood. Rather they were shamed and castigated for becoming mothers. This denigration was emphasised when their identities were hidden by the issuing of a replacement birth certificate from which their names were excluded. Refusing mothers and adult children access to adoption information is yet another strategy in this process of maternal alienation.

Adopters, on the other hand, are often objects of pity, if they are unable to have children. They are also viewed as having performed a community service by being brave and generous enough to give a home to a child who is perceived as lacking a family. If rearing an adopted child becomes at all difficult, as it frequently does, then the adopters may be seen as both the victims of the child's behaviour and the heroes who tolerate it. Of course, the mother is rarely physically present in the lives of adopted children and so is unable to correct the negative image of her, which has been created by her absence. Many mothers report that the separation from their children has left them feeling isolated and punished.

Maternal alienation– long term outcomes

a) in relationships where abusive fathers are involved

The effects on children of maternal alienation are many. Often they are unable to view their mother as a loving and nurturing parent. Their trust in loving relationships in general can be undermined. They may become trapped in the view of the situation which has been presented to them by the abuser, lacking the ability to understand the strategies which have been used. Because of the undermining of their relationship with their mother, they may be unable successfully to create intimate relationships in adulthood. If the children challenge the abuser's view of the mother, they are often blamed and accused of being disloyal.

Such children are growing up in a situation where the roles and relationships are false and not based in reality. This prevents them from healing from the separation from their mother. The abuser is, in fact, putting his needs before the needs of his children and so the children find themselves relating to a parent who does not have their best interests at heart. The result of this is often that the children find themselves trying to meet the needs of the abusive parent.

The effects on the mothers are that they often adopt the view of them which has been presented to their children and blame themselves for the estrangement. Mothers feel isolated and alienated from friends and family. Mothers feel enormous grief and pain at the loss of the close relationship with their children. They often feel powerless, as they have a sense that they are unable to have any impact on the situation. Mothers suffer emotional trauma because of the loss of the relationship with their children and this undermines their confidence in themselves. As a result they often find it difficult to refute the accusations made against them.

b) in relationships where adoption is involved

The parallels with adoption are very clear. In the same way that mothers and children are abused by maternal alienation perpetrated by some fathers, they have also been abused by the maternal alienation perpetrated by adoption. The system of adoption itself (although not necessarily the individuals involved) has been guilty of perpetrating maternal alienation by creating an estrangement between mothers and their children. Those mothers and children have suffered long term effects of that estrangement.

Many adopted people have grown up feeling abandoned and rejected by their mothers and so, of course, it is often impossible for them to view her as a loving and nurturing parent. The relationship between a mother and child at birth is the closest and most basic of all human contacts. When this relationship is interrupted and not allowed to develop after birth, then the child may be so damaged that he or she becomes unable to develop intimate relationships in later life. Because their emotional survival, growing up as adopted children, depended very much on accepting the definition of family with which they were presented, they have seldom been able to understand the strategies that have been employed to alienate them from their mothers. Any attempt to challenge this narrow view of family (ie restricted to the adoptive family) is often met with accusations of disloyalty.

Adults who have grown up in adoptive families have often internalised the false relationships which adoption attempts to create. Their definition of family roles and relationships, therefore, is not based in reality. If they are able to challenge this definition and accept the reality of their relationships with family members, then they risk being accused of being disloyal to their adoptive family. Many adopted adults choose to limit their close relationships to the bonds which were created at the time of their adoption and lack the courage to attempt to add to those relationships by recognising the reality of their actual relationships with their families. By imposing those restrictions upon themselves, they are retarding their own healing, not to mention the healing of their mothers, who are also victims of this practice of maternal alienation. Adopted people often underplay the impact of adoption separation in their lives, as they are afraid that acknowledging it would render them frighteningly vulnerable.

Many adopters are more concerned with their own fears than they are with the emotional well-being of their adopted children and actually support the alienation of their adopted children from their mothers by discouraging, either overtly or covertly, the interpersonal healing which the reunion might bring. Sadly, many adopted adults feel responsible for what they perceive to be the emotional well-being of their adopters and they act in a co-dependent role by supporting them in avoiding reality and retarding healing.

Mothers often adopt the view of themselves which has been created by society and feel guilt and shame. They frequently blame themselves for the separation from their children and feel isolated and alienated from family and friends. They feel enormous grief and pain at the loss of their children along with a sense of powerlessness to address the issues. This powerlessness is emphasised when they are prevented from having information which would allow them to contact their adult children. The emotional trauma which they suffer often has a negative impact on their self-confidence for many years and so they find it difficult to defend their positions.

Because of the maternal alienation which has been practised and the lack of recognition of the abuse suffered in this way by adopted people and their mothers, it is often particularly difficult for adult adopted children and their mothers to form a close bond at the time of reunion. Other relationships, such as those between siblings, are often less fraught.

One of the principal tasks of reunion between a mother and adult child is for an understanding to be gained as to how this alienation took place, in order that the rift can be healed and the estrangement reversed.

I believe that the maternal alienation which occurs as a result of adoption is damaging to both child and mother, but that it cannot be avoided, no matter how the adoption is arranged. It can only be avoided by creating alternatives to adoption. It is possible to arrange for children to be cared for in ways which will not result in maternal alienation.

How does the grieving experience change over time?
The first three months after the loss event (death or reunion), often pass in a daze, as the feelings seem overwhelming. During this period, our thoughts tend to be centred on our loss. After the first three months, those involved often begin to have a sense that life is regaining a degree of normality. The first anniversary of the event is also very significant and it can be beneficial to the healing process for it to be marked in some way. In some cultures, for example, it is only after this first year has passed after a death that the gravestone is erected. After two years have passed, there is an easing of the original anguish and after a ten year period has passed it is unlikely that there will be major changes in the relationship (either with the deceased or with the family member with whom reunion has occurred).

After a death, what often happens is that the bereaved person gradually starts to adjust to the loss and has some happy moments, but then they feel guilty for being happy and so they draw back into their grief again. In reunion, people also often reach out and then draw back. This is sometimes because they feel guilty and unsure. In both situations, those affected are having difficulty adjusting to the change and retaining a sense of loyalty and commitment to the previous way of life ie prior to the death/reunion. This kind of behaviour in a reunion relationship can be very frustrating for the other party involved.

Grief can be re-triggered at any time by external events or by memories. Revisiting our grief from time to time can be a useful experience and is not necessarily a negative behaviour. Providing our grief feels manageable and is not preventing us from enjoying what life has to offer, we can allow it to have a place in our lives without feeling guilty. The sadness which comes over us at the time of the actual event, eg a death or other major separation, often is of a deeply anguished nature. When we revisit that event some years later, however, the grief which we experience then usually has more reflective, gentle qualities.

Reunion and fathers

It seems trite to state that every child, adopted or otherwise, has a mother and a father. In adoption situations, however, not only have fathers tended to be reluctant to come forward, but many mothers have also been reluctant to draw attention to the fathers of their children. As a result, the role played by fathers in adoption reunions and the impact of adoption on the lives of fathers has received little attention in adoption literature.

Fathers of adopted children fit into several categories. In some cases the father was closely involved with the mother throughout the pregnancy and was involved in the events which led to an adoption outcome. In some cases, the father knew about the pregnancy, but the relationship broke down before the birth and the mother was left to manage her situation alone as best she could. In some cases the father never knew that he had helped to create a child.

With regard to reunion, there are issues for fathers themselves and there are issues relating to fathers for mothers and adopted adults.

For many of the fathers who knew about their children, the long term issues have been very similar to the issues for mothers. Many fathers have felt guilty about not supporting their children or the mothers of their children and have carried the shame related to that guilt for many years. For those fathers, being contacted or being able to contact their adult child, provides the same valuable opportunity to explore and experience their grief that the contact does for mothers. They can heal the hurts of the past and try to build a relationship with their child. In some cases these fathers are the ones who initiate contact.

Mothers and fathers who have lost children to adoption are often in a position to offer to each other a great opportunity ie the opportunity to address their grief issues and perform their personal recovery work. If this occurs prior to reunion with the adopted adult, then that adult will have the benefit of being reunited with parents who have explored and experienced their grief and are therefore more able to support the adopted adult child.

For those fathers who were not aware that they had helped to create a child, there has been no opportunity to involve themselves in any kind of preparation and so the contact will invariably take them by surprise. Whether or not he is ready to accept the fact, a father is a father and as such is entitled to be offered the opportunity to confront the reality of his position.

In almost all cases of fatherhood, there exist, in addition to the father, members of the father's family, who are relatives of the adopted adult. In my view it is right and proper that those relatives be offered the opportunity to welcome the adopted adult as a family member. As a grandmother, I cannot imagine how painful it would be to know that one of my grandchildren had grown up without being able to acknowledge me as a grandparent.

At the time of reunion, some adopted adults discover that they have two parents who are still in touch with each other, perhaps even married. Some adopted adults find a mother who carries nothing but anger towards their father. Some adopted adults are informed that their father is unaware of their existence. In some cases mothers refuse to give any information about the child's father.

In many cases, therefore, the adopted adult is dependent on the mother for information about the father and for assistance in locating him. So many mothers delight in the generosity of their children to include them in their lives. However, it is tragic that there are also many who fail to show the same generosity towards either their child or the child's father and refuse to co-operate in helping the child to trace the father. I hope that these mothers will reconsider their position. It is never too late.

For mothers, part of their personal recovery involves coming to terms with the reality of the circumstances of conception. In some cases the identity of the father is unknown or there is more than one person who could have fathered the child. Exploring and understanding these circumstances is an important part of the mother's personal healing. Accepting that her child has received not only her own genetic contribution but also that of the father can be difficult for some mothers, but it is a necessary part of their personal recovery work.

Often any feelings towards the father, which the mother has buried over the years, will come to the surface at the time of reunion. It is wise, therefore, for mothers to take the initiative and try to acknowledge and address those feelings as part of their recovery work. In some cases it may be possible to contact the father and address any unresolved issues before undertaking any steps to contact the child. For many mothers this is a vital part of their preparation for reunion. It sometimes happens that when parents come into contact with each other again, there is an inclination to resume the relationship which they feel was interrupted by the pregnancy.

Regardless of any issues between the mother and father, the child is part of the father's family and sometimes that child is the only grandchild of the father's parents. They may have been unaware of the pregnancy and played no part in the adoption process. They may be delighted to know that they are grandparents. Regardless of their response to the news, it would be respectful to their position for them at least to be advised and then placed in a position to make an informed choice, regarding how they respond to the news.

The father may also have other children who can be made aware of their sibling. They too will then be in a position to make an informed choice, regarding how they respond to this information. Making a decision deliberately to withhold such important information from family members cannot be supported. It would be unfair and disempowering, not only to those family members, but also to the adopted adult child, for those choices to be withheld from them.

Hopefully, all of those whose lives have been affected by adoption can come to understand, that there is much to be gained from the inclusion of fathers in the reunion experience.

Part III
Questions

Chapter 1
Questions asked by parents

I've thought of searching for the son I gave up for adoption but some people are telling me that it would be selfish of me to contact him. I don't want to ruin his life by intruding. Do I have the right to do that?

Every adopted person (those who have had the benefit of knowing that they were adopted, that is) knows that they have a mother and a father. Every adopted person knows that there is a possibility of a reunion with their mother and/or their father. Some have anticipated those events and have chosen to prepare themselves and others have chosen not to prepare themselves. You have no way of knowing how ready your son might be to meet you again, but you will be doing him a great favour by allowing him to know that you care about him. In my opinion, you would be acting in your son's best interests by contacting him and allowing him to make an informed decision about the opportunity you are offering him. I don't think that making contact with your son would be selfish. In fact, I believe it is a very generous act. ***I am quite sure that my son and I would never have found each other had it not been for the fact that we had both chosen to search.***

Some people say that adopted people who search for their parents mostly just do it out of curiosity and that they usually only want information, not a relationship. Do you think that's true?

I believe that family members who have been separated by adoption seek each other with a view to improving their level of emotional well-being. Not everyone is aware of this, of course, at the time of making the decision to search. Many people say after they have been reunited that they didn't understand why they had searched until after the reunion had taken place. Adopted people often say that they search out of curiosity and that's true. At a very basic level, that's what it is. On a deeper level, however, I believe that they are seeking a more complete sense of self, which can be achieved by addressing the impact of adoption on their lives. They are often afraid to say that they would like to have an on-going relationship as they don't want to be disappointed if it doesn't eventuate. I don't feel that it's useful to ask people why they search for their family members, unless you are going to use that information to help them to explore their experiences and motivations. In my view it is a quite understandable aspect of human nature to want to seek out those to whom we are related. So many people research their family histories because they feel that knowledge of their ancestors contributes to their self-knowledge. People also seek out family members from whom they have been separated, even when no adoption has taken place. As adults, we choose which family connections we wish to nurture and maintain.

It's wonderful to have my daughter back in my life, but sometimes I feel that I'm the one making all the effort in the relationship. I get tired of it. Why doesn't she make an effort to show me that she's interested?

You have to remember that, although you are both adults, you are the parent in this relationship. You have a conscious memory of the closeness which you and your daughter once shared, while she does not. You have had the opportunity of more years to experience life, to mature and to prepare for this reunion. As the parent, you will always have those advantages. Parents are generally expected to set an example for their children. Adopted people sometimes find it difficult to accommodate their complex family ties. Just remember that she doesn't owe you anything and that any contact you have with her is a bonus. I have never understood why some people seem to think it's useful in relationships to keep a mental record of who initiates each contact. I don't see that there's anything to be gained by keeping score. I would suggest that you try to be glad that you know her and enjoy the time you have with her.

I was reunited with my daughter some years ago and her life is a real mess. She's very demanding and her constant crises are affecting my life, my health and the other members of my family. I just feel that I can't cope with this any more. I've been told not to walk away from her as she will feel as if she's been abandoned twice. What should I do?

It's very difficult to be reunited with a family member and to find that their values and their way of life are very different from your own. It is often easier for us to be tolerant towards the children that we have raised, because we knew them and can remember them when they were innocent and vulnerable. With a child we did not raise, it is often more difficult to set boundaries. So many parents feel that somehow they have to try to make up for the fact that they allowed their children to be adopted and they fear that if they withdraw support from their adult child, then that child will disappear out of their life again. Only you can decide firstly, at what point you have given so much and can give no more and secondly, to what extent you are helping your child or perhaps instead supporting her in a lifestyle that is not conducive to her own well-being. It's also about creating some kind of balance among all of the relationships which exist in your life and finding a place for this one where it will sit comfortably and not overshadow the others. In the initial phases of reunion, this is often what happens, but after some time there is usually a reduction in the original intensity. This allows those involved to have more emotional energy to devote to the other important people in their lives. When this happens you will not be abandoning her any more than you did when she was adopted.

I gave up two sons for adoption. I just don't know how I'm ever going to explain that either to them or to the daughter I raised. I can't quite come to terms with it myself and when I've tried to tell other people, they find it very hard to understand.

There are many parents who have lost more than one child to adoption. The factors which were operating at that time are often complex. It's possible that there was a degree of loyalty to the first child, that would not allow you to raise the second. If adoption was presented to you as being 'the right thing to do' for your first child then why would it not also be 'right' for your second child? It's probable that little, if anything, had changed in your circumstances, to persuade you to think any differently. It shows how powerful the forces in favour of adoption were at that time, that you could have been persuaded to repeat the procedure. It's also very likely that you had not grieved the loss of the first child and were really not in a healthy emotional state to be dealing with a second pregnancy. There was also a familiarity about consenting to adoption, because you had experienced it already. When we're under stress, our behaviour tends to revert to familiar patterns. Losing a child to adoption often results in low self-esteem, because of the guilt and shame involved. If you were feeling worthless after the loss of your first child, then how could you be expected to have the confidence that you could raise a second child competently? I'm sure there were many contributing factors which led to this outcome for you. It would be useful for you to explore them, perhaps with professional help, in order that you can accept and understand your experience and then you will be more comfortable sharing it with others, including your children.

I gave up my daughter for adoption because I was told that it was the 'right' thing to do. Then later I was blamed for not raising her myself. I'm confused now. Did I do the 'right' thing? Would I still have been blamed if I had done the 'wrong' thing?

I think many mothers were in a 'no-win' situation in which there was no 'right' choice. We had no way of knowing what the long term impact of our decisions would be. Adoption was presented as the 'right' thing to do because it was felt to be in the best interests of our children. We were often made to feel that we deserved to suffer (for our 'sins') and that raising our children would be selfish, yet I have never heard of a mother who was blamed for not having given away her baby. I believe that by becoming pregnant when we did, we challenged the expectations of society at the time and so others tried to make us feel inferior and inadequate. In fact, I believe that we were trailblazers and that we played our part in forcing our societies to confront the fact that a woman was not the possession of a man, to be 'given away' by one man (her father) to another (her husband). I hope that single parents today recognise that their freedoms were largely built upon the sufferings of others in earlier decades.

I received a telephone call from a social worker when I was at work, telling me that the son I had given up for adoption wanted to contact me. I just panicked and said she must have the wrong person and terminated the call. I was shaking and had to go home. I think it was really inappropriate for her to call me at work like that with no chance to prepare myself, don't you?

I agree with you completely. The way in which the contact information is passed on is really important, yet, sadly, some intermediaries handle it in very insensitive ways. I'm sorry to hear that contact was made in this way and hope that you will be able to have direct contact with your son in the very near future.

All through the years that I didn't know what had become of my son, I thought about him all the time. However, his birthday was always the most difficult day for me. Now that I've met him, I still find myself feeling sad on his birthday. I don't want to spoil the day for him. Have you any suggestions to help me?

Many parents find it helpful, whether they have been reunited with their children or not, to set aside some time on their child's birthday to honour their parenthood and their feelings for their child. This can be useful for adopted people also, as they may feel a degree of sadness on their birthdays. Their birthday, after all, is an annual reminder that they were not raised with the families into which they were born. It is usually best to set aside some time for this early in the day as that can allow you to approach the remaining part of the day with a more positive attitude. Some people light a candle, or even bake a cake. Some write a statement or a poem. Some recognise the significance of the day in their journal. You can be creative and invent your own form of ritual to mark the occasion. If those affected by adoption separation can deliberately set aside a time in the day to acknowledge their experience and their loss, then it is less likely that their feelings of sadness will intrude on the remainder of the day.

When I was reunited with my son, my parents wanted to meet him too. I was really upset and didn't want to share him with them, especially when they were the ones who made me give him away in the first place. Do you think they deserve to meet him?

For many mothers and sometimes also fathers, their anger with their parents resurfaces at the time of reunion. Looking back, it seems to many that their parents were harsh and judgmental and could have done more to help keep the child within the family circle. However, if our children can be generous enough to understand the position we were in when they were born, I think we can try to understand how it was for our parents. It might be helpful to your healing if you spoke to your parents and tried to understand their motives and intentions at the time your son was born. Hopefully you can work through some of your anger, so that your son can benefit from the love and caring that they have to offer.

I decided that it was time I started talking about the son I gave up for adoption and so I joined a support group. It's a mixed group and has members who are parents, adopted people and adoptive parents. I came home from the first meeting feeling very distressed at some of the comments which were made. I don't think I'll ever go again. Do you think it's important to go to a support group?

Attending a support group can be very helpful, but that's not to say that every support group meets the needs of its members. I suggest to everyone that they try a group. My personal view is that the purpose of a support group is for those who are facing a particular issue to meet with others who have shared the same experience, such as having been separated from a child by adoption, in order that they may support each other. I know it can be valuable to learn from those who have experienced adoption separation from a different position, but I do not believe that a support group is the appropriate environment in which to have such an interaction. I think it's advisable to trust your judgment with regard to what is helpful for you. Support groups are not for everyone. It may be that the support group environment does not suit you, but you may meet people there with whom you could form your own personal support network. While it can certainly be very valuable to talk to others who have had the same experience, this does not necessarily need to happen in the formal setting of a support group meeting, or even in the confines of a support organisation.

I decided to try to find the son I gave up for adoption, but by the time I managed to trace him he was already dead. I am devastated and angry and feel as if I've lost him twice. I felt guilty before about giving him up, but now I feel even more guilty. Perhaps I should have looked for him sooner. Perhaps his death had something to do with the fact that I didn't raise him. How can I ever deal with my grief when the possibility of reunion has been denied me?

This is a tragic outcome and I am very sorry that you have lost your son. There are no easy answers to your question. I believe that insightful counselling could help you to come to terms with the circumstances which led to the adoption. Also your anger is quite appropriate, but I believe it is important that you don't turn it inwards on yourself. Perhaps you can find a way to 'get to know' your son through the people who did know him. Is it possible for you to have some memento of him or to visit his grave? Perhaps you could create your own ritual to acknowledge his death and your motherhood. You are not responsible for your son's death and I hope that you will find someone supportive who can help you to manage your grief.

I was told by a social worker that the daughter I gave up for adoption wants to contact me. I'm fifty-two years old and I have a good husband who loves me dearly but I've never told him about that child. How can I tell him that I've lied all these years? I just couldn't face the past coming back into my life now. Surely at my age I should be protected from this kind of thing?

It must have been a terrible strain for you to keep your daughter a secret for all those years and it may not be easy to acknowledge her existence now. In fact, she has never been in the past, as you have carried the thought of her with you for many years now. Imagine what a relief it will be to be honest finally and to release yourself from the tension of hiding the fact that you had a child who was adopted. Secrets are corrosive and destructive in relationships because people are not living with reality – instead they are trying to avoid it. They are unable to accept their true selves; to love themselves as they really are. The path to emotional well-being requires honesty. It's wonderful that your daughter wants to know you and this is a great opportunity for you to express your feelings and be true to your motherhood.

'Protecting' yourself from the truth in a situation like this is actually condemning yourself to on-going deceit and stress. You may find that your husband will be relieved to know the truth, as he may have been aware of your reactions to certain events over the years, for which he had no explanation. Adoption reunions often raise deep emotions for those involved and it's a time when you need the support of those who love you. If you and your husband have a close relationship, then I'm sure that he will continue to love you and that he will be happy to support you in your reunion with your daughter. If he really loves you, then he'll love you for who you are, not just who he thought you were. How could the man who loves you not care about a child who is yours? I'm sure he will appreciate that you have trusted him enough to give him a realistic picture of who you are, one which includes the fact that you have a daughter. It may not be easy in the beginning, but once you have faced the truth, I'm sure you'll wonder what it was that you feared so much.

I've been reunited with the son that I lost to adoption but it's been rather a stormy relationship over the years. Then recently he met his father. Since then he seems like a different person. He is much more accepting and less judgmental. Have you heard of this happening before?

Yes, I have. It's an interesting phenomenon. It seems that some adopted people (men in particular) find it difficult to accept that their mothers allowed them to be adopted. Somehow, hearing the same story from their father makes all the difference. I always hope that mothers will be able to see that there are many benefits for all concerned in supporting their children to contact their fathers.

I wrote to my son but he didn't write back. I waited three months and then wrote again, but there was still no response. I know he's living there because I have a friend who knows the family. Don't you think he at least owes it to me to let me know that he's alive and has received my letters?

I don't think adoption reunions are about people 'owing' anything to each other. I don't see it as being about obligation. Legally he doesn't owe you anything, although some people might think he has a moral obligation to you. If he chooses to respond to you, then I'm sure you'll be delighted. Many people are not prepared for contact and it takes some time before they are ready to respond. I hope that you can be patient with him but not give up. He may be dealing with other issues in his life at this time, of which you are unaware. You have offered him a priceless opportunity but he may not be ready at this stage of his life to accept your offer graciously. In the meantime, it is your responsibility to take care of your own recovery, regardless of his behaviour.

I'm the father of a child who was given up for adoption. I never saw my daughter when she was born and yet I thought about her and missed her for thirty years, before I finally contacted her. Does that surprise you?

Not at all – in fact it seems perfectly normal that a parent would continue to care about their child, regardless of the lack of contact between them. Parents who are separated from their children by divorce, for example, continue to care about their children. I'm delighted that you were able to let your daughter know that you cared for her and hadn't forgotten her.

I would like to contact the daughter I lost to adoption and I've been advised that the best way to do this is to use an intermediary. I can't forget how the social worker treated me when my child was born and don't want to trust a social worker again to make contact with my daughter. Do you think it's always better to use an intermediary? How can I find one that I can trust?

No, I don't think it's always better to use an intermediary. People must do things in the way that feels right to them. Intermediaries can cause serious problems in relationships or they can help things to run smoothly. There is no way of knowing how the use of an intermediary will turn out. Some people resent the intrusion of an intermediary. Using an intermediary is always risky, but then making contact is, by its very nature, a risky activity. Supposing your daughter tells the intermediary that she does not want to hear from you, then you may have lost your only opportunity to hear directly from your child. Intermediaries, whether friends or professionals, often have their own views and values around adoption and could influence your daughter against contact with you. I would suggest that you plan carefully how you intend to make contact, trying to make the experience as comfortable as possible for your daughter. There may be a trusted family member you could ask to act on your behalf rather than a social worker, or you may decide that the best way would be to contact your child yourself. Only you can decide.

We married after giving up our son for adoption. We met him again when he was eighteen years old and he was surprised to find that he resembled our other children. This puzzled us as we expected our children to look alike. Can you explain this?

It's difficult to understand the degree of denial that exists around adoption situations. I am frequently amazed by the comments that I hear. Some adopted children grow up absorbing this denial to such an extent that a thirty-year-old adopted man I spoke to was worried about his hair loss, because his adoptive father went bald at an early age. One adopted woman said that she did not expect her mother to be short like her, as everyone in her adoptive family was tall. These people are living in an unhealthy fantasy world with an astonishing degree of denial. They seem to have acquired these attitudes because of the community denial that surrounds adoption.

I gave up a daughter for adoption. She was conceived as a result of a rape experience. I thought that I had put the experience behind me, but then I got a letter when she was thirty years old saying she wanted to contact me. I saw a counsellor over a period of some months and found the counselling very useful. I hadn't realised that I needed to grieve the loss of my child. Finally I felt that I was prepared for meeting my daughter. However she has been very rude and angry towards me since we met and now I wish that I had never met her. I know I can't go back and change what has happened, but I feel that, as long as I told myself she was happy and had had a good upbringing, then I was able to live with it all. Now I find that the thought of her and the way she behaved towards me just makes me unhappy. I feel that it would have been better for me if the meeting had never taken place. How can I learn to live with what has happened?

I can understand that it has been very painful for you to have been subjected to your daughter's anger and resentment. It's unfortunate that she behaved in that way towards you. However, the fact that she did contact you drew your attention to your need for support in your grieving and this has been very useful to you. While it may have felt more comfortable, in some ways, to have held on to the fantasy of how your daughter's life might have turned out, you are now forced to deal with the reality. While you have to accept her as a person, you do not have to accept her rudeness. Many adopted people are angry, as are many parents, but there is no justification for expressing that anger in hurtful ways towards a family member. I suggest that you express clearly to your daughter that you love her and care about her, but stress that you expect to be treated politely by her and make sure that, as the parent, you model the type of behaviour which you would like her to exhibit. Hopefully your daughter will also seek appropriate help and find ways to explore and express her feelings, which do not involve insulting and hurting other people. As you say, you cannot turn back the clock. The reunion has been a great opportunity for both of you to address the issues which the adoption separation has brought to your lives. You can make sure that you make the most of that opportunity, but you cannot dictate how your daughter will use her opportunities. Please be patient, remember that you are the parent and don't give up hope that she will grow in understanding and compassion.

I read your book *Adoption and Loss – The Hidden Grief* and I thought it explained really well how we were not able to grieve the loss of our children when they were adopted. Do you think if we had had community support at the time and been able to grieve, that everything would have been fine?

It seems to me that those women who did get some help at the time of the separation from their children and were able to grieve to some extent have shown fewer on-going signs of repressed grief. However, because of the lack of finality of the loss, I believe that it was not possible for us to complete the grieving tasks at the time of separation, in the way that we may have done following a death. The reunion experience provides a type of finality and I believe that this is part of the motivation to seek to have a reunion. Also I believe that we don't really know what it is that we have lost until our children are adults and so there is an element of the grieving which cannot be addressed early in the separation. The bottom line is that I don't believe that there is any painless way to separate parents from their children.

My husband and I have recently found the son that we gave up for adoption before we were married. He tells us that he already has a mother and father and cannot bring himself to call us by those names. Is this normal? Is he in denial? How can we reach an agreement on what he should call us?

You are his mother and father and nothing can change that. The names which we give each other do not affect the nature of our relationships. Adopted people belong in one way to their adoptive family and in another way to the families of both their mothers and their fathers. However, I'm sure that you can reach an agreement with him on the issue of naming. My advice is to discuss it with him openly and calmly and remember that you are the parents. I suggest that, for now, you be guided by your son, safe in the knowledge of your relationship to him, which cannot be affected by the titles he chooses to give you. Some people have more than one person in their lives to whom they refer as 'mother' or 'father', in the same way that I have several people in my life to whom I refer as 'son'. Also remember that your son's wishes in this respect may change over time and the best that you can do is to keep the channels of communication open. Be happy that he wants to include you in his life. I told my son once, 'You can call me anything you like, just don't stop calling me.'

After I gave up my daughter for adoption, I was treated for depression. Now I've met my daughter again and I feel that the depression is coming back. Do you think I should take medication again?

First of all, I'm not a medical person and so I don't give medical advice. I do not believe that adoption outcomes should necessarily be considered to be mental health problems, but I suggest that you discuss any health concerns you have with your doctor. However, I believe that in a lot of cases where an adoption separation occurred, genuine grieving was mistaken for depression, because professional people did not recognise the adoption separation as a loss situation. It's possible that in some cases the medication actually helped to suppress the grief and so that would explain why it seems so often to come to the surface again later in life and especially at the time of reunion. This can be true for adopted people as well as their parents. I believe that reunion often brings up the grief which was not allowed to be expressed at the time of separation and that, for that reason, being sad is often an appropriate response to an adoption reunion.

Unfortunately, again, many professionals do not understand this and suggest medication for a condition which, in my opinion, is not an illness, but serves a useful purpose. Reunion also can bring up feelings of anger and when anger is turned inwards it can present as depression. Once people understand that reunion reactivates the dormant grief, they are better able to manage their emotions. A little piece of information like that can make all the difference to how we deal with the situation. My little grandson, for example, thought that I could perform magic when I was able to make his toy train carriage move without touching it. One day he'll understand about the use of magnets and know that the train moved, not because his Grandma had magical power, but because of the laws of physics.

Even though it's been two years since I met my son, I still feel anxious that he'll walk out of my life again. I couldn't bear to lose him twice. Because of my fear, I find that I often hold back when I'm talking to him, as I'm afraid of saying the wrong thing. I can never really relax. Will it always be like this?

Many parents describe that feeling of 'walking on eggshells' because of their fear of somehow offending their child and then losing contact. For most people, a time comes when they feel comfortable enough to be themselves and say what they feel, with only the usual restrictions, in terms of good manners, that we employ in our dealings with other family members. It's impossible to predict when that time might come. However, rather than put yourself through so much stress for fear of what might happen, it might be better for your general well-being to try to relax more when you are in your son's company and trust him to accept you and understand your feelings for him. The relationship will continue if you both want it to continue and it is unlikely that he would terminate it after two years on the basis of one misunderstanding or disagreement. Maybe the relationship could actually be strengthened by being tested, rather than being restricted to what feels to you like 'safe' behaviour. If you show him that you are able to accept him for himself and allow him to be honest, then you are demonstrating to him the kind of behaviour which you hope he will exhibit towards you. Only you can decide whether you would rather continue to feel so constrained, or are prepared to take the risk of being yourself and letting your son respond to you in his own way.

I want to be more open about the daughter I lost to adoption, but I don't know how to tell people. What should I say?

You can practise using whichever words feel comfortable for you. You might want to bring it up when you meet a new person and they ask if you have children. People sometimes say, 'I have three children, two daughters and a son, but my son was born before I was married and I was persuaded that he would be better off if I gave him up for adoption.' Some say, 'I have three children, but I was able to raise only two of them. My first child was taken from me to be adopted.' Some say, 'I had one child, a son, but I lost him through adoption.' You can experiment and find which statements you feel represent your experience and your feelings and try them out, until eventually the information will be easy to share. Every time you talk about your child as being a part of your family and a part of your life, you are acknowledging the truth and owning your experience. You may also be educating another person and helping to increase community awareness of adoption issues.

I've never felt sad about giving up my daughter for adoption as I think it was the best thing for everyone concerned. I don't see that I have any need to grieve. I did cry a lot after they took her away and over the years when I didn't know what had become of her, but now that I know she's had a good life, I don't think adoption is really something to grieve over. Why do you think people can benefit from grieving over something that has turned out all right?

It's interesting that you say that you didn't feel sad about the separation from your daughter and yet you shed many tears. Crying is certainly one way to grieve and possibly the most common way of expressing grief. No matter how the adoption seems to have turned out for both of you, there has been a separation of mother and child and there have been losses experienced. Many people have buried their feelings of loss and so their grief, when it does occur, takes them by surprise. Some people, however, have been able to acknowledge and express their feelings (for example by crying) and so for them much of the grieving has already been accomplished before they find out what the outcomes of the separation have been for the other party. Anecdotal evidence suggests that those who have had those opportunities to grieve cope better with reunion, because they are more prepared for it by having already addressed, to some extent, their loss issues. When your daughter was adopted, no one knew if it would 'turn out all right'. I think that the grieving is about the separation and the loss, regardless of the outcomes. It may be that if your daughter had had an unhappy life as an adopted child, then there may have been more grief for you on learning of that.

I've been reunited with my son but his wife seems to be so jealous and it seems that she would like me to disappear out of his life again. Is this normal?

It's certainly common but not at all what I would call 'normal'. Strong feelings occur around adoption reunion but many of them are neither healthy nor productive – nor are they in any way inevitable. However, you need to be mindful of the fact that your son's first loyalty is to his partner. It would be good for you to acknowledge that and to avoid any situation in which he might feel that he has to choose to please one or the other of you. Also, be patient and undemanding and allow your relationship to develop at its own pace, bearing in mind that he needs to find a place in his life for all of the people who are important to him.

This is not an easy task. However, many people's lives these days are complex and they manage them quite comfortably.

I am a father who lost a child through adoption. I recently met my son and was horrified to be told by him that he was abused by his adoptive parents and removed from their home under child protection legislation. How could this be allowed to happen? We were told that adoptive parents would give our child all the advantages which we were unable to give him. Why didn't they contact us when this happened so that we could have brought him up instead?

Yours is a tragic story and what is even more tragic is that it is not as uncommon as people would like to believe. Many adopters did not have the skills and the commitment to be able to raise children, especially the children of others. Sadly, in many cases, this did not prevent them from being given the care of other people's children. Those children have suffered, firstly from having been adopted and secondly from having been abused. It is heartbreaking for parents to discover that their children did not, in fact, receive all of the expected advantages in their adoptive families. Hopefully you can now have some positive input into your son's life and help him to heal the hurts from the past.

I've met my daughter but I find it difficult to feel close to her. How is it that she seems to be so relaxed with my other children?

Relationships between siblings often lack the tension inherent in relationships between parents and adult children who have been separated by adoption. This tension may be partly caused by the maternal alienation that is involved in adoption. If you and your daughter can explore that and see how it has happened, I'm sure that will help you to build your relationship. Meantime, I hope that you can enjoy and appreciate the fact that your children are close and be patient and allow your own relationship with your daughter to grow over time.

I've met the child that I gave up for adoption but I've never been sure who the father was. I've told my daughter that I can't remember anything about her father, because I am too embarrassed to admit that I was promiscuous. I only want to protect my child from being hurt. Do you think I've done the right thing?

I think that there has already been too much deceit and denial involved with adoption. I hope that you can feel comfortable enough with your daughter to be honest with her. Your use of the word 'promiscuous' is interesting. I rarely hear men describing themselves as 'promiscuous'. Perhaps some counselling would help you to explore your behaviour in the light of the judgmental attitudes of the time when double standards created a lot of shame and guilt for women.

I've met the daughter I gave up for adoption and we get on well together. Everyone thinks I should be happy now but I still get very sad sometimes when I think that I gave her up and was not able to be a mother to her. Will I ever get over it?

I don't think it's about 'getting over it'. Of course you will always have some sadness related to the separation from your daughter. I think that's perfectly natural. When those times arise, I suggest that you just let yourself experience those feelings and know that they will pass and that they will not prevent you from having a contented and fulfilling life. We all have events in our past which we revisit from time to time; some are sad events and some are happy ones. Just be glad that you are able to get in touch with your feelings and experience them. They're your feelings and expressing your feelings is not as big a problem as not being able to express them. It's a question of finding a place for those feelings in your life and not allowing them to overshadow the good feelings you have about your daughter. Your relationship with your child will always have an element of sadness, in the same way that emigrants, no matter how much they appreciate the benefits of life in their chosen destination, often live with a sense of what has been lost. You are her mother and you brought her into the world. That's a contribution of which you can be very proud.

I've been reunited with my son but my parents refuse to meet him. Is that common?

Yes, it is common. Older people tend to be less adaptable and sometimes find it difficult to assimilate 'new' family members. Also, many grandparents were instrumental in arranging the adoptions of their grandchildren, or at least did not prevent those adoptions from taking place and so the reunion often brings up feelings of guilt and loss for them, which they sometimes wish to avoid. Hopefully their attitudes will change over time.

I've met the son that I lost to adoption but his adoptive parents were not happy about us seeing each other. They told him that he was not allowed to mention me when he was with them. So because of the tension this caused, he saw less and less of them and then they started to say that I had ruined their life and turned him away from them. Is there any way that he can get them to be more generous and understanding?

After an adoption reunion takes place, what usually happens is that the people involved become more aware of themselves and more confident in who they are. This often gives them a sense of freedom. Inevitably, this affects their relationships with other people. Once people like themselves better and understand themselves better, they relate more honestly and openly to other people. Often this means that relationships are strengthened, but not always. It seems that your son's adopters feel threatened by your presence in his life. I hope that they will learn to accept that he has a place in all of his families, otherwise they may be the ones to drive him away.

A few years after I lost my daughter to adoption I spent three months in a mental health facility with what was termed at the time a 'nervous breakdown'. When my daughter became an adult, I was terrified that she would want to contact me. I thought that if I had to revisit all that pain, I may have another breakdown. We met, however and I didn't have a breakdown. In fact, it has been a joyous and wonderful experience. Do you think my earlier breakdown actually served a purpose?

It's certainly possible that what was termed a 'nervous breakdown' was actually your way of trying to process your grief. It may be that when you were reunited with your daughter, the grief which arose was thereby made more manageable. I have heard of many parents who have suffered breakdowns between losing their children and being reunited with them, sometimes triggered by another loss event. Often no connection is made between the breakdown and the adoption separation, but it may well be that your grief forced itself to the surface and made you deal with it in the early days, thereby saving you from going through that degree of anguish again at the time of reunion.

Since our reunion, my daughter has made it very clear that her adoptive parents are much more important to her than I am. She rarely contacts me and seems to expect me to be grateful for the small amount of time she condescends to share with me. I'm finding this more and more hurtful as time goes on and I'm wondering if it would be better for me not to see her at all, rather than being constantly reminded that she clearly considers me second-rate compared to her adoptive parents. Would I be wise to break off all contact with her?

Your feelings are not uncommon. It might be helpful for you to spell out your feelings to your daughter (perhaps in a letter) clearly and without blame. You may want to reassure your daughter that you care about her and want her to be a part of your life, but that certain aspects of the current situation are making you feel unhappy. You run the risk, of course, of alienating your daughter and then not hearing from her at all. Only you can decide if the situation is such that you are prepared to take that risk. As family members, we each have our role to play but there is not always agreement on what that role will be. Remember too that in families where there has been no adoption, parents are sometimes dissatisfied with the amount of time allocated to them by their adult children. Once our children become adults, they lead their own lives and make their own decisions. Where there has been an adoption-related separation, of course, the issues are more complex because the expectations of both parties to the reunion might be quite different. There are many parents who don't even know if their children are alive or dead and there are others whose children refuse any contact at all. Perhaps you might find more contentment if you are able to enjoy the contact that you have with your daughter without being disappointed that you do not have more of her time. It may also help if you are able to appreciate your relationship with your daughter for what it is, without comparing it to other relationships which she has.

My wife and I gave up our first child for adoption. The only way we could live with that decision has been to convince ourselves that we did the right thing. I'm terrified that if we try to contact our child, we might find out that we didn't do the right thing for him after all. What would you advise?

In my opinion, it's not about whether or not the adoption was the right thing or the wrong thing, a good thing or a bad thing. If your son has been happy and well-cared for and grew up with an acknowledgement of his adoption issues, that does not necessarily mean that the adoption was a good thing or the right decision. On the other hand, if your son was abused in the adoptive family, returned to care by the adopters or if the issues associated with being adopted were not addressed, this was not necessarily because the adoption itself was the wrong thing. Your decision was made with good and positive intentions but with no knowledge of what the outcomes would be. I think that you would be helping yourselves and your son to work towards resolving all of your adoption issues by making contact with him and confronting the truth.

When I was reunited with my son, he wanted to get in touch with his father. The three of us met together and I realised that I still have feelings for my childhood sweetheart. However, I'm happily married. Am I just fantasising or is it possible that I married the wrong man? Is it too late to do something about it? Does this happen often?

As far as I am aware, there are no statistics to show how common your experience is. I do know, however, that this does happen sometimes. Adoption reunion is an emotional time and those involved are very vulnerable. The reunion often causes the emotions which were experienced around the time of pregnancy and birth to resurface. Sometimes there has been a great deal of anger between the mother and the father which has simmered for many years. This can erupt at the time of reunion. Sometimes there was a great deal of affection between the mother and the father and that too may have continued to exist, although deeply buried, for a long time. The reunion often causes those warm, affectionate feelings to come to the surface. It may be that your relationship with your son's father was prevented from running its course and so you have a sense that it was unnaturally broken off and remains somehow incomplete. Just be aware that this is a time of deep emotional turmoil and not a time to be making important decisions. Try to be patient and focus on yourself and your own feelings as well as building a relationship with your son. Your feelings about yourself and your feelings about your son will have an effect on all of the other relationships in your life. Many mothers feel that they have not truly been themselves since the separation from their child and the reunion brings a great sense of relief and often a feeling of having permission once again to be themselves. This newly-found emotional freedom can cause some mothers to behave recklessly. Rather than making rash decisions, I would suggest that you find someone independent and trustworthy with whom you can discuss your feelings and adopt a wait-and-see policy, until the emotional turmoil has settled somewhat.

Why do adopted people sometimes object to their parents referring to them as their 'adopted child'?

I don't know. I have five adult children. They will always be my children, no matter how old they (or I) become. They are my sons and my daughters. Your child is your child in the same way that your mother is your mother, regardless of how old either one is. Our children become adults and then they are our adult children. The key point is, though, that parents discuss with their children how they prefer to be described and that they reach an agreement on the matter.

So many adopted people seem to express a lot of anger towards their mothers and/or fathers. Is it mostly the ones who have had negative experiences in their adoptive families who react in this way?

Hostility is a common component of grief and grief often comes to the surface during adoption reunions. Many adopted people are angry and many of them direct that anger towards their mothers and also sometimes towards other family members. In my experience, many adopted people who display intense hostility towards family members also claim to have had a happy upbringing in their adoptive families. Sometimes the way they express their anger is by refusing contact with their parents. If adopted people can explore and understand why they are so angry, this can improve their level of emotional well-being and help them to build relationships with family members.

I know that losing a child to adoption is in some ways like experiencing a bereavement, but I also know that I dare not say that to people who have experienced the death of a child. I am afraid that they will tell me that their grief is worse than mine because they know that they will never see their child again. Which do you think is worse, death or adoption?

I don't think it's helpful to compare the two experiences. I don't think it's possible or useful to say that one type of loss is greater or has a deeper impact than another. Everyone's losses can be acknowledged. One of the problems with adoption has been that, until recently, it was not recognised as a loss experience. We suffer many types of losses throughout our lives, through death, the ending of relationships, emigration and ill-health among others. It's important that we educate the community to understand that parents did suffer from the loss of their children who were adopted. I believe that this is more likely to be achieved without such comparisons.

My son who was lost to adoption has come back into our lives but I find that my other son, whom I raised, seems to be jealous of his brother. Is this normal?

Such jealousy is certainly common but not at all what I would call 'normal'. It may take some time for your family to accommodate your son, who has been absent for so many years. Be patient and try to be cautious and considerate of the effort involved in adjusting to this new situation. In any family there are those who are close and those who are not. Parents have to accept that.

I've been reunited with my daughter but she's been terribly spoilt and expects to be treated like a princess. I'm sure she wouldn't have been so selfish and self-centred if I had raised her. Why did this happen?

Sometimes adopters have tried to protect the adopted child from hurt, as they see it, but have, in fact, prevented the child from growing and developing in the way that most of us do, by dealing with adversity and learning to be resilient. Sometimes they felt that they had to give the child everything (eg telling the child that they are 'special' and 'chosen') to make up for the child having lost his or her families. As a result some adopted children have grown up expecting to receive everything they want with little effort on their part and are not prepared for challenges or adversity of any kind. On the other hand, studies with identical twins separated at birth suggest that their inherent personalities have had more impact on their lives than the environments in which they were raised. You'll never know how much of your daughter's behaviour is a result of her personality and how much is a result of her upbringing. While, to some extent, it would make it easier to build a relationship if you are able to accept her for who she is, I think it would also be appropriate for you to discuss with her what it is about her behaviour that concerns you and to set your own boundaries.

I want to contact my daughter but I've been told that I am not allowed to have her contact details and that I must make any approach through a social worker. I find this really degrading and unnecessarily intrusive. Why do they make laws that demean us in this way?

I agree with you that it is degrading and insulting for you to be treated in this way. I have no idea why such laws apply. I can only guess that there is some fear that parents who have lost children through adoption can't be trusted and would somehow act in ways that would be harmful to their adult children. Of course, there is absolutely no basis for such fears. Weren't we the ones who supposedly acted in our children's best interests to allow them to be adopted in the first place? Unfortunately, some of the social workers who operate in this area are less than ethical in their work and yet many parents are at their mercy. In South Australia, parents have had access to identifying information about their adult children since the Adoption Act (1988) was passed. I see no reason why such legislation could not be enacted in every other location in which adoptions have taken place. I hope that you will soon enjoy direct contact with your daughter.

I've been reunited with my daughter and after our reunion I wrote a letter to her adoptive mother, to reassure her and to explain that I understood that she was my daughter's mother and that I could never replace her. Did I do the right thing?

That's hard to say without having read the letter. I'm not sure why you thought that your daughter's adoptive mother might need such reassurance. If, in your letter, you supported her in believing that, as your daughter's adoptive mother, she has some kind of superior claim to motherhood than you do, then I don't think that that is going to be helpful to her. Did she write you a letter, for example, saying that you are your daughter's mother and that no one could take your place? In my view, adoption is not about anyone replacing anyone else, it's about people acknowledging the reality of everyone's place.

My wife and I have been reunited with the daughter we gave up for adoption before we were married. She was happy to hear from us but said that if we had left her alone, she would never have looked for us. I've heard that only about a quarter of adopted people search for their families. Is this true and if so why do you think it is? Do you think this means that the other three-quarters are quite content without a reunion?

First of all, it's impossible to know how many family members separated by adoption are able to be reunited, as many do not use official assistance. If anyone tells you that they know what percentage of adoptions result in a reunion, then they are misleading you. Some adopted people will say that they had never thought of searching but, in fact, by not searching they had, by default, made a decision not to search for their parents. Some adopted people fear that their parents will not welcome them into their lives. Some don't want to stir up their own buried feelings of loss. Some feel that they have nothing to offer. Some are angry with their parents and don't want to offer them any part of themselves. In spite of the fact that they have chosen not to take an active role in the search process, however, many adopted adults are delighted to have been contacted by their parents.

It's been wonderful to meet my son again, but it seems that being with him brings back all my hurt and sadness from the time he was born. It's hard to enjoy being with him when all I can feel is the pain, especially if he talks about his childhood or his adoptive family and I realise how much I have lost. Will I ever get over this and be able to enjoy spending time with my son?

I think it's vital to the future of your relationship with your son that you manage to address your sadness in ways that do not interfere with the building of this relationship. Of course, meeting your son again will bring up deep feelings of loss and grief for you. It is likely that these feelings have not been addressed and it is certainly in your best interests to explore those feelings and to experience them. However, I hope that you can find a way to do that, which is separate from the time you spend with your son, so that he does not feel that he is causing your sadness. It's not him, nor the reunion with him which is causing your hurt and sadness. It is the original separation which has caused your pain. Please try to find a way to work through that grief so that you can go on to enjoy fully the precious gift of having your son in your life.

I'm so ashamed of having allowed my child to be adopted. I feel that somehow I should have been able to prevent it. Will I ever get rid of this guilt?

Yes, you can. I sometimes wonder what caused such shame in so many women. It seems to me, looking back, that pregnancy leading to marriage was not so shameful, but pregnancy that didn't lead to marriage was usually very shameful. Apparently there were priests in Ireland who used to say that pregnancies usually last nine months, but 'first babies can come any time' (meaning any time after marriage, of course). I think that a lot of women were ashamed that they became pregnant to men who either refused to marry them or whom they did not want to marry. In order to release yourself from that shame, you can focus on the reality of your situation, try to understand how and why it happened and accept that you acted with good intentions. You can find a place in your life for your adoption experience and be proud that you are a parent and that you brought a child into the world. You can work out how to make sure that the pain from the past does not prevent you from having joy in the present. You deserve to be happy.

I recently found the son that I gave up for adoption. Now I suspect that he is sexually involved with my daughter (his half-sister). I'm horrified. How could this happen?

Siblings who have been raised together have usually learned that brothers and sisters are not appropriate candidates to be sexual partners. Siblings who have been raised apart, however, have not had the opportunity to absorb these attitudes towards each other and the barriers which normally grow in families do not exist between them. This is compounded by the fact that those who were adopted as children have grown up among people who do not reflect them physically and they tend (often subconsciously) to be seeking such people and to be attracted to partners who resemble them. When they meet relatives, who do reflect them physically, they are often drawn to each other in a physical as well as an emotional way. This can also occur between parents and children. Usually, if those feelings exist, they are not acted upon. As the relationships between family members grow and develop and the initial intensity subsides, they usually come to realise that sexual behaviour such as this is inappropriate.

I've managed to contact my daughter, but she has refused to meet me because she thinks it will upset her adoptive parents. I'm really angry with them for raising her to believe that she should be responsible for their comfort. How can any kind of parents encourage their adult children to deny themselves valuable opportunities just because the parents think it would make life more complicated for them?

I know that there are many adopters who have made it clear to their adopted children that they would not be happy if they had a reunion with their parents or other relatives. However, I also know that there are many adopted adults who make their own decisions regardless. It may be hard for you to accept, but your daughter is an adult and has made her own choice. If she has really been unduly influenced by her adopters, then she has allowed that to happen and, as an adult, must take responsibility for that. Hopefully she will come to see that a reunion with you would be a valuable learning experience for everyone involved, by allowing them to confront reality.

My son refuses to tell his children who I am, because he does not want his adoptive parents to know of our reunion. His children don't know he's adopted and think that I'm a friend of the family. I hate to see my grandchildren being raised with lies and secrets. How can I persuade him to be honest with them?

This situation, sadly, is not uncommon. It's very hard to see the secrecy and deceit associated with adoption being carried through into another generation. Perhaps you could explain to your son that you value the truth and do not wish to be involved in deceit. I hope that he will see the wisdom of openness and honesty. Adopted people who do not tell their adopters that they have met their family members, are denying them the choice of whether or not to share that important experience with their child. Adopters have always known that they were raising someone else's child. They have always known that there was a possibility that the child would be reunited with the families of origin, although they may have chosen not to prepare themselves or their child for that event. Are you able to discuss it with his wife? Perhaps she could talk to him about this. In the meantime if you concentrate on building a strong, close relationship with your son and his family, then when he is able to live with the truth, you will be there to provide support.

My son was adopted but it was an open adoption and so we had some contact over the years. I was told that this would mean that he wouldn't have the same issues which adopted people have who were raised without any contact with their families. Now he's an adult and he tells me that he feels that he doesn't belong in either family. Do you think that the contact was of any value?

There are not enough children who have been raised with so-called 'open' adoption arrangements like these and who are now adults, for research to have been conducted which would give us any indication of the long term outcomes. From my own experience of talking with parents whose children have been raised with some contact with their families, the issues for these children are very similar to the issues experienced by those who were raised without contact with their families. Mothers have told me that their children, as they approached adolescence and began to understand the position in which they found themselves, sometimes became resentful towards their parents, whom they saw, at that stage of their lives, as being relatively mature and prosperous. These adolescents had difficulty understanding why their parents had chosen not to raise them. In many situations, also, arrangements for contact were made but contact ceased a short time after the adoption took place. Sometimes contact was broken off by the parents, who found it too painful. Sometimes contact was broken off by the adopters, who found it too threatening. Anecdotal evidence suggests that children raised with contact will still suffer from the loss of their position in the family and that parents who have been separated from their children through adoption, even when they have had a degree of contact, will still suffer from the loss of their parental roles in the lives of their children.

My daughter searched for me and found me. It was a huge surprise but I was delighted that she wanted to know me. Everything went really well for the first three months and then all of a sudden she turned on me, was really angry and hurtful and said that she never wanted to hear from me again. Why did she bother to look for me if she was only going to walk out of my life again?

Adoption reunions tend to rekindle feelings of loss and grief related to the original separation. Hostility is a common component of grieving behaviour following a bereavement and so is the inclination to try to escape from the truth and pretend that the death has not really happened. Similar behaviour also occurs sometimes after an adoption reunion. Your daughter may also be dealing with other issues in her life at this time, of which you are unaware. Try to be patient with her and allow her time to work through her grief. Remember too that you are the parent. She may not fully comprehend what it is that she is experiencing and may feel lost and afraid, as many people do during their grieving, whether they are grieving a death or another type of separation. She may have felt when she searched for you that she wanted to have you in her life forever, but ***no one can predict what they will***

experience after the reunion has occurred*. It may not be easy, but perhaps you can find a way to reassure her of your feelings for her and at the same time allow her the opportunity to work through her own feelings. Her behaviour is common in adoption reunion experiences and many reunions survive this sort of phase. I know it's difficult to deal with, but, hopefully, if she knows she can rely on you not to give up on her, she'll move through this phase and it will become a learning experience on which both of you can build.*

I've been sending my daughter a birthday card and Christmas card every year for five years and have never had a response. Should I give up?

I have heard of adopted people who were delighted to receive such correspondence, even though they have never responded to it. At least you are able to write to her and she has accepted your mail. Many parents are unable to do even this. Because of your efforts, your daughter can never deceive herself into thinking that you don't care about her and hopefully one day she will respond in some way. I hope you won't give up.

I gave up my son for adoption and I would love to find out how he is and maybe even get to meet him. However, people are telling me that that wouldn't be fair to his adoptive parents and that I should think of them and stay out of their lives. What do you think?

Your son is an adult and he is the one you need to consider, not his adopters. Many adopters are delighted when their adopted children are reunited with their families. I believe that you would be doing all of them a favour, by making a considerate approach. Your son will make his own decisions.

I'm a father who recently was reunited with my daughter, who was given up for adoption twenty years ago. I'm really sad about all the years we've missed spending together and angry at the way my feelings were disregarded when she was born. My daughter, however, seems to be very cool. She never talks about her feelings or tells me that she cares about me. I find it very hard to connect with her. What do you think she's experiencing? Are things likely to change?

It's impossible to know how much of your daughter's behaviour reflects her personality and how much of it is a result of the impact of adoption separation in her life. Many adopted people are cautious and fear abandonment. As a result they tend to be undemonstrative and to avoid commitment. This is their way of protecting themselves against what they might perceive as a rejection. It would be helpful for you to read about the impact of adoption on adopted people, as this might help you to understand her better. Remember also that people show their feelings in different ways and be glad that she is obviously keen to spend time with you. Not everyone is comfortable with expressing their feelings in words. In contrast, there are also people who are very clever with words, but there is actually no depth of emotion behind their words. If your daughter has welcomed you into her life, then that is evidence that she cares about you. Be patient, be yourself and allow the relationship to grow and develop over time. Also it would be useful for you to be able to explore your own feelings around the adoption and to manage them in a way that does not interfere with the relationship with your daughter.

I've tried to contact my adult daughter, whom I lost to adoption, but the social worker has been told by the adoptive parents that my daughter does not know that she is adopted. Because of this, the social worker has refused to help me any further. What do you think I should do now?

First of all, I think it is appalling that you are at the mercy of a social worker and that this person has the right to make these sorts of decisions. If your daughter has been deceived up until now, then anyone who supports that deceit is, in my opinion, acting unethically. Deceiving your daughter is insulting and demeaning to her and is also preventing her from grieving her loss and addressing her adoption issues. I hope that you can find some other way to contact your daughter and release her from the constraints placed on her by those who choose to lie to her and prevent her from knowing the truth about herself and her families.

My son was not well-treated by his adoptive parents, who had very definite expectations of him which he failed to fulfil. Yet he still seems to show a strong sense of loyalty to them. Is this common?

Yes, it is. Sometimes it seems that because adopted people felt that they had been abandoned by their original families and therefore cannot trust them, they will not dare to take the risk of alienating their adoptive families, in case they find themselves with no family at all. I met one young woman who was adopted and she was placed in an orphanage by her adoptive father after her adoptive mother died when she was five years old. She had met her parents, but told me that her 'primary allegiance' still lay with her adoptive family. Sometimes it just seems too big a risk to take to criticise the adopters in any way. This may be very frustrating for you, but I don't think it would be useful for you to challenge what he perceives as loyalty. I suggest that you concentrate on your relationship with your son and make sure that he knows that you love him unconditionally.

My child was taken from me and adopted and I don't feel that the proper procedures were followed. If this is true then the adoption was illegal. Surely somebody should be made to answer for that?

I know that some mothers feel that they were not treated fairly when their children were adopted. I think that many of us were so traumatised by what was going on, that it would be very difficult now for us to be sure of what transpired at that time. Many of us were so anxious and distressed, that it would have been difficult for us to comprehend and absorb what was being said to us. Also many mothers have blocked out details of their experiences over the years in order to protect themselves. I think it's more useful to look at the bigger picture and to try to understand why all of those adoptions took place when they did. I think it's important also that we deal with what has happened, rather than focus on what could have happened or should have happened. I'm not convinced that looking for someone to blame helps anyone's healing. There's the danger of such behaviour degenerating into a kind of witch-hunt and that focussing on other people's behaviour may prevent an honest exploration of our own. In the end ***we are all responsible for our own healing, regardless of the actions of others****. It's a complex issue. Certainly it's helpful for the community to be made aware of what happened, but I don't think it's helpful to anyone involved for mothers to be portrayed as helpless victims, nor for them to appear to be vindictive and vengeful*.

I am the father of a child who was lost to adoption. My name was not on the original birth certificate but I would like to know my child. Is there anything I can do?

Your options are dependent on the legislation in the area in which your child was born. In some places fathers are entitled to be given identifying information about their children. Your first step might be to contact the government authority or adoption agency involved and find out what your rights are. In some places there is a contact register where you might be able to place your name. You may even be able to have your name added to the original birth certificate. Another option might be to contact the child's mother and see if she would be willing to assist you. I hope that you are able to make yourself known to your child and that your child appreciates your efforts.

My son was conceived through rape. I've considered searching for him just to find out if he's all right, but I'm terrified that he will have turned out to be like his father or that if I meet him it will bring back the horror of my rape experience. Do you think I'd be better to leave well alone?

From my experience, children conceived through rape are just as precious to their mothers as children conceived in other circumstances. You may find that if you meet your son, it will be clear to you that he is a unique individual and not just the product of a disempowering, abusive event. It would probably help if you first of all work through the issue of being a rape victim with someone who specialises in that area and then work at understanding your responses to the adoption separation, before you take the step of trying to contact your son.

Why did you write about your personal experience in your book *Adoption and Loss – The Hidden Grief*? I lost my child through adoption and I refuse to tell my story publicly because I think it only provides more ammunition for the people who want to blame us.

I told my story to illustrate my views on adoption loss and grief, to encourage other mothers who had had similar experiences to be open about those experiences and to educate the community in general. I believe that I have achieved all of those aims. I wanted people to see how the circumstances into which I was born, the historical era in which I grew up and all of the events in my life led up to the loss of my child and how the grief from that loss remained unexpressed for so many years. I hoped that people would make those connections and that it would help them to have a better understanding of why so many births did result in adoptions and why so many mothers suffered from losing their children. I am proud of the many brave parents who have told their stories publicly and I know that they have had a huge impact on adopted people and on the community in general. I have been contacted by many mothers who told me that reading my book helped them to understand their own experiences and their own feelings. I've also been contacted by many adopted people who have told me that after reading my book they have a much better understanding of what their mothers have suffered. Many professionals working in the post-adoption area have also expressed their appreciation. A great deal more community education is needed and in my opinion anything that brings adoption issues out into the open and encourages honest and productive discussion is helpful.

I don't understand adoptive parents. How could they just take someone else's child? I could never do that.

How many times have you heard someone say, or dreaded hearing someone say, 'I don't understand people who give up their children for adoption. How could anyone just give away their baby? I could never do that.' ? There is nothing inherently wrong in wanting to give a child a home. Many adopters believed that they were doing what was best for the children. When our children were taken from us to be adopted, we didn't understand the implications and the far-reaching consequences of that event. Adopters also did not understand the implications for themselves and the children they were adopting. All adopters are not bad people any more than all parents who lost children to adoption are bad people. To understand how and why so many adoptions happened, it is useful to explore people's motives and intentions. I don't think it's useful to look for somewhere to pin the blame.

I decided that it was time I started to tell people about my daughter and thought that it would be wise for me first of all to try to understand how and why the adoption happened and the impact it may have had on both of our lives. I managed to read lots of books about adoption. However I found that many of them were very directive, telling me what I 'should' be feeling and doing.

Not only that, but they often contradicted each other. How can people work out which books are the best ones to read?

I understand exactly what you mean. It can certainly be helpful to read of the experiences and opinions of others, but I would look very carefully at the credentials of the authors you choose and try to discover if they have any hidden agenda. Some books don't seem to help people to deal with the complexities of their experiences. There is also the danger that some authors do not have a deep understanding of the dynamics of adoption separation and reunion and may completely misunderstand and therefore misrepresent what is happening. Sadly, there are also authors who examine the hurt caused by adoption but also promote adoption as a positive outcome for families. In my opinion, if they really understood the issues resulting from adoption separation, they could not possibly encourage more people to become involved in adoptions. I encourage people to read as much as they can, but also to try to rely on their own judgment more than anyone else's. Be very wary of any author who tells you what you 'should' be doing or feeling or what you 'must' do. Remember that each adoption experience is unique and try to find perspectives that feel right for you. In the end we are each responsible for our own decisions.

I've met my son but I feel really guilty because I don't like him. He is selfish and irresponsible and I find it really hard to relate to him. However I adore his children and it's been great to develop a relationship with them. How can I learn to accept him as he is?

There are many parents who don't approve of their children's behaviour, whether they raised them or not. Perhaps you can focus on the fact that you want what's best for your son and continue to try to encourage him to make the most of his opportunities in life. That's wonderful that you are able to be part of your grandchildren's lives and hopefully you can have a good influence on them and enjoy the time spent with them. You would not have had that if the reunion had not occurred.

Most adoptions took place in the 1960s and 1970s. Social workers at that time knew that mothers and their children suffered serious emotional consequences after being separated by adoption, because academics had written articles about it. Surely they had a responsibility to warn us instead of trying to persuade us to consent to the adoptions of our children?

When I published Adoption and Loss – The Hidden Grief, *I stated in the final chapter that in my view there was no excuse for any further adoptions to occur. Just because I wrote that, however, doesn't mean that everyone now 'knows' that to be a fact. Many people have not read my book. There may be some who have read it, but do not agree with me. I expressed my opinion. If articles were written expressing the opinion that mothers and their children would suffer as a result of adoption separation, that doesn't mean that anyone 'knew' that to be the case. It only means that someone expressed that opinion. Prior to the mid-sixties there were too few adoptions on which to base any reliable research and it was uncommon for mothers to come forward to describe their feelings. This means that there was no 'evidence' on which to base such opinions. The view in the community in the decades in which most adoptions took place was overwhelmingly that children would be disadvantaged by living with one parent rather than two. This view prevails to a large extent today. In fact, for most mothers, the reactions of their parents and the fathers of their children to news of the pregnancy had a much greater impact than the views of social workers. If either the father or their parents had been supportive, most mothers would never even have met a social worker.*

I am a mother who lost a child through adoption. Now that we have been reunited, my son wants to know about his father. I love my son dearly, but why should I help him to find his father now, when he abandoned me during my pregnancy and refused to take any responsibility? He caused me nothing but heartache and I don't want him back in my life. Why doesn't my son understand how hurtful this is for me?

Adopted people have two parents, like everyone else. Many mothers hope that their adopted children will want to know them. Why would they not want to know their fathers too? Mothers who lost children through adoption were usually young and disempowered. Many years later, when those children are adults, the mothers they are meeting have matured and grown in awareness and understanding. Mothers can exercise the same courage and generosity which their children have exhibited in being reunited with them, to give fathers the same opportunity to gain awareness and understanding. Many fathers have carried the guilty burden of having abandoned the mothers of their children. Many mothers have lived with secrecy, stress and denial, not facing reality - they would be doing the child's father a favour by releasing him from the same experiences. They would also be doing their children a great favour if they can help them to locate their fathers. I think your son, as an adult, is entitled to make his own choices with regard to a relationship with his father. Do you really think you are treating him fairly by trying to prevent the possibility of such a relationship by withholding information?

Chapter 2
Questions asked by adopted adults

Adopted people are really the innocent parties in this whole adoption business as we had no say in what took place when we were born. Don't you agree that because of this we should be able to make the decisions when it comes to search and reunion?

In my view it is unfortunate that people sometimes talk about adopted people as the 'innocent' parties to the adoption. This feeds into the notion that others (eg mothers and fathers) were in some way the 'guilty' parties. I don't think that this is helpful. I think it is more helpful to rid adoption of notions of guilt and blame altogether. What were your parents 'guilty' of – of wanting the best that life could offer you? In fact none of us, whether adopted or not, had control over what happened when we were born. No one, at the time of their birth, chooses how or by whom they are going to be raised. Adopted people are no different from the non-adopted members of the population in this regard. It's what we make of our lives that's important. Adopted adults make their own decisions about reunion, as do parents, but I do not believe that they have any superior right to decision-making over anyone else involved. I am quite sure that my son and I would never have found each other had it not been for the fact that we had both chosen to search.

I was recently reunited with my mother. It's been a really difficult time for my adoptive mother as she has always felt that she was my only mother and now she feels that my mother is trying to replace her. Is there any way that I can help her to make the adjustment?

There is no replacing of parents taking place in adoption. Your parents are your parents. In some families, there are people other than parents who raise a child and act in a parental role. They may be grandparents, adopters, foster parents, stepparents or anyone who cares for and raises a child, whether or not they have legal custody. The people who raise you, whether or not they are your parents, have a unique place in your life. When children become adults, their relationships with those who have had parental roles in their lives have to be renegotiated. When a reunion takes place between a mother and child who have been separated by adoption, the mother will not replace the person who has acted in a maternal role in her absence. Each person has their place and their role in your life. If your mother does not raise you, then the person who does will have a place in your life in addition to your mother, not instead of your mother. For example, if your mother died and your father remarried, your stepmother would not replace your mother, she would be an additional mother figure in your life. For some people, they have a mother who after a period of time is no longer there to care for them (whether through death, adoption or separation of another kind) and then there may be other maternal figures in their life. They do not have to end their relationship with one, when they begin a relationship with another. Your mother will always be your mother even if she is physically absent (through death or separation). The same applies to fathers. Your father is your father whether he participates in your upbringing or not. There may be other people in your life who act in a paternal role and you may care deeply for them, but that does not change the facts. Hopefully your adoptive mother can come to understand that she has a unique place in your life, as does your mother.

I've met both of my parents and discovered that they were married a few years after I was adopted and have three more children who are my full siblings. They are still married and they seem to be such a happy family. I feel really cheated that I wasn't able to be a part of that family as I was growing up. I feel as if the other children were important enough to keep but I wasn't. Can I ever get over my anger with them for giving me away and then staying together?

The fact that your parents are still together can be seen as an advantage, in one way, in that it means that you get to meet your father and mother together. It also shows you that you were born into a deep and loving relationship. I'm sure it's very painful for them to confront the fact that you were raised separately from their other children, but the past cannot be undone. I hope that you can begin to find your place in your family and enjoy the warmth that is there. Anger is common in reunion relationships and it's important that you find productive ways to express it, without it preventing you from building a strong relationship with your family members.

My original mother wants to meet me. I want to tell her that I'm quite happy and I already have a mother. How can I get that across to her without hurting her feelings?

To be honest, I can't imagine how any mother could hear that kind of message and not be deeply hurt by it. When your mother agreed to your being adopted, I'm sure she was hoping that you would be raised by adopters who would love you unconditionally and foster an awareness in you, that you had parents who loved you and cared about you, before they did. In my opinion, as a mother, it would have been heartbreaking if I had found that my child did not recognise me as his mother and did not want to know me. Had I had to face that response, I would have felt doubly distressed, because I gave him up for adoption and because he was refusing to acknowledge his identity and heritage. I hope that you'll reconsider and find the courage and generosity to be able to offer your mother a place in your life. Please give yourself some time to consider the situation more deeply. I feel there is a lot to be gained for you by including your mother in your life.

My mother wants me to visit her and sleep at her home. I tried that once before and it just made me feel really strange and emotional. I can't understand why, but I don't want to do it again. How can I tell her this without hurting her feelings?

Other adopted people have also told me that it affected them deeply to sleep under the same roof as their mothers. Some have even felt that they wanted to sleep in the same bed with their mothers and this has scared them. Because of these feelings, some adopted people refuse invitations and then misunderstandings arise. I think it's all part of adjusting to the fact that your mother was not present during your childhood and so you are both struggling to establish a relationship for which there are no socially accepted norms. I think it would help if you are able to talk to your mother about your feelings so that you are working on this issue together, instead of allowing it perhaps to turn into an area of conflict. Otherwise your mother may assume that you do not care about her and she may stop issuing invitations. Over time, I'm sure these feelings will gradually become less intense. Your relationship with your mother does not have to meet any set standards. It belongs to you and her and it is up to both of you to build the kind of relationship which you both want to have.

I've been reunited with my mother and my father (who are both married to other people) and now I find that my life is so complicated. My adoptive parents have divorced and have both remarried and so now I have four sets of 'parents' to accommodate and fit into my life. What should I call them all? What will my children call them? Is it possible to keep everybody happy? Who should take precedence?

Because so many relationships in our times do not last a lifetime, many people are dealing with complex family situations.

Children are interacting with half-brothers and sisters as well as with people who might be known for example as 'my mother's boyfriend's daughter'. Children are able to work out who is related to whom and where everyone fits. Appropriate naming can be achieved by negotiation. No one automatically has precedence and it can be tricky to juggle the various family relationships with which we must deal, even where there has been no adoption in the family. However, we manage, because that is the way our lives are.

I've been contacted by my mother, but I feel that there are some issues that I want to sort out before I'm ready to meet her. I really want to know her, but I'm worried that she won't like me as I am and I want to take some time to make changes. Do you think she'll understand this and be able to wait until I'm ready?

I hope that your mother will be able to be patient with you and allow you to move at your own pace. However, you don't have to be perfect before you're ready to meet her. It would be helpful for you to think about why you feel that you are not acceptable as you are. I hope that you have read some books about the impact of adoption and have had the opportunity to discuss adoption issues with someone who is familiar with the area. Hopefully your mother will be able to accept you for who you are, her son, in the same way that you feel you want to know her because she is your mother.

I'm adopted and I was raised in a family which had a different racial and religious background from the one into which I was born. On the one hand it was obvious as I grew up that I was adopted and so there was no secrecy, but on the other hand, the obvious physical differences between my adoptive family and me made me feel isolated and alone. It has also made it very difficult for me to relate to the racial group into which I was born, as I am ignorant of their language and culture. Are there others like me who feel that they just don't fit anywhere?

Sadly, there are many people like you who have been raised in a racial and cultural environment in which they have felt out of place and among people who did not reflect them in any way. Many adopters did not understand what the implications of these differences would be for the children they were adopting. Thankfully, there are fewer of such adoptions now, but there are still many, like you, who are living with the aftermath of the policies which allowed this to happen. I hope that you will be able to meet with others who have had similar experiences and that you can learn to assimilate your adoption experience into your life. I also hope that you will be able to acknowledge your true value, as an individual with a unique mix of cultural influences.

I've read a lot about the shame felt by mothers who lost children through adoption. I have grown up being ashamed of being adopted. Is this common? I always felt that I was second-best because I was given away by my parents. How can I get over my shame?

It's very sad that your parents most likely thought that they were saving you from the shame of illegitimacy by allowing you to be adopted, yet you have felt shame because you were adopted. Perhaps it would help if you try to take control over the information about your adoption, rather than allowing others to make you feel ashamed of it. You could find ways of explaining that you were adopted that feel positive and comfortable to you, such as saying, 'My parents were very young when I was born and they thought that they couldn't provide for me. They wanted me to have the best in life and so they allowed me to go to my adoptive family', or 'My mother was single when I was born and she didn't know where to go for help. The social worker convinced her that adoption was the best outcome for me.' Such explanations emphasise that the motivations which led to your adoption were positive and that the adoption happened because people cared about you and not because they didn't care about you. Being raised apart from your families does not mean that you are inherently flawed in any way. Reunion helps people to own and accept their history so that the element of shame can be removed. Some people, sadly, choose to continue to live with shame. By not acknowledging the adoption, adopters often actually foster a sense of shame in their adopted children. Secrecy and shame go hand in hand. Events of which we are proud are rarely kept secret. It might also be useful for you to learn about the experiences of parents who lost children through adoption, so that you can see how and why so many adoptions occurred. Hopefully we can educate people and rid adoption of the curse of guilt and shame. I also believe that it is not helpful for adopters to be made to feel guilty or ashamed for having adopted. There's nothing inherently wrong with offering a home to a child who seems to need one. Nor is it helpful for parents to feel guilty and ashamed for the fact that someone else raised their children. In most cases they believed that they were acting in the best interests of their children. There is nothing wrong with wanting the best for your child. Adoption has obviously had a big impact on your life, but it's still possible for you to reach a stage where you are comfortable with who you are. Counselling might help too.

I'm adopted and I had been thinking about searching for my mother one day. However, she contacted me and took my choice away from me. I'm so angry that I had no choice when I was born and then I didn't have any choice about being contacted by my mother. Why couldn't she have left it up to me to make that decision?

Well, no one has any choice when they are born and it seems to me that your mother has not taken anything from you. In fact, she has given you a great opportunity. All she did was let you know that she cares about you and that she is there for you, if you choose to meet her. You still have a choice. I hope that you can learn how to deal with your anger so that it will not interfere with the relationship between you and your mother. Many adopted people would be delighted if their mothers made themselves available for reunion.

I was reunited with my father recently and since our meeting he has showered me with gifts. He wants to take me on holidays and buy me a car. I appreciate his generosity, but it makes me feel very uncomfortable as it's almost as if he's either trying to buy my affection or else trying to make up with his money, for not being there for my mother when I was born. I don't know if he's kind to me because he cares about me or if he's just trying to ease his conscience. How can I explain this to him and ask him to back off a bit, without appearing rude or ungrateful?

Parents who have been reunited with their children often feel that they want in some way to 'make it up' to them. For some parents, who have the financial means, one way to try to do that is to spend money on their children. I'm sure your father enjoys buying you gifts. He may see it as trying to make up for all the lost years, rather than trying to make amends for his behaviour. Hopefully, as you get to know each other better, you will feel more able to express your feelings honestly to him and be able to let him know that these extravagant gifts make you feel uncomfortable. I'm sure that's the last thing he wants to do. It would be better to be honest rather than withdraw and let him assume that you do not enjoy his company. Perhaps you could reassure him that you are happy to have him in your life and that time spent together is the most valuable gift he can offer.

I was very surprised when I was reunited with my mother as I realised that some of the feelings I was having were similar to the feelings I had when my close friend died. On both occasions I felt numb and disbelieving, then overcome with sadness, then angry at what had happened. I'm wondering if there is any connection between adoption and death?

Many people describe similar feelings surrounding a death and an adoption reunion. In fact, being involved in an adoption reunion is like experiencing the death of the dream, or the death of the 'not-knowing'. The two experiences can certainly result in similar feelings and it's good to understand that, so that we can accept that how we feel is appropriate. Then we are able to move through those phases of grieving and hopefully come to a point where we are able to assimilate those loss experiences into our lives.

I read an article about post-reunion attraction and it really scared me. It seems that in a lot of adoption reunion situations, sexual relationships develop between family members. I'm thinking about searching for my mother and I'd hate to find myself in a situation like that. Is there any way I can make sure that doesn't happen?

I've been involved with family members separated by adoption for fifteen years. I've travelled extensively and have counselled many people who have been reunited with family members following an adoption separation. In all that time I have not met one person who told me that they had become sexually involved with a family member following an adoption reunion. While in many cases there is a feeling that reminds people of romantic attraction and while there is sometimes a desire for physical contact, actual sexual relationships in adoption reunion situations are very rare. It's important to be aware, if you are hoping to have a reunion, that the feelings may be very intense, especially in the early stages of the reunion. If you prepare yourself for this, then hopefully you will be able to manage any feelings which arise. The vast majority of reunions do not result in inappropriate sexual relationships.

My mother tells me that she had 'no choice' but to give me up for adoption and that she 'didn't stand a chance' against her family, the social workers etc. I find it hard to believe her as she seems to me to be a very strong and assertive woman. Sometimes I think that she's just trying to make up excuses. How can I know if she's being honest with me?

First of all, it would be helpful for you to try to gain some understanding of the situation your mother was in at the time of her pregnancy. Her life experiences since that time and the way she has approached them may have allowed her to develop into a strong and assertive woman and for that I think she is to be applauded. However, at the time of your birth it is unlikely that she was able to assert her wishes. It might be helpful for you to read material written by those who experienced society's disapproval at that time, or talk to other people who found themselves in similar situations. That way you might learn about the factors which allowed some women to be mothers, while others became mothers who lost their children through adoption. Many societies have traditionally frowned upon mothers who sought to raise their children without fathers and often the mothers, rather than the fathers, have come to be blamed for such situations. Until Federal Government financial support for single parents was introduced in Australia in 1973, for example, it was almost impossible for a single woman, unaided, to provide financial support sufficient to raise a child alone. Even after government support became available, the social stigma and the resulting perceived disadvantage to the child deterred some mothers from attempting such a daunting task. Some mothers definitely did not have a choice. In some places, for example, if the mother was under age at the time of the pregnancy, her parents had the legal jurisdiction to make a decision on her behalf. Some mothers were deceived and were not given accurate information which could have allowed them to make an informed choice. Some mothers feel that they did exercise a degree of choice but that their options were so limited as to appear to be no option at all. Others believe that they thought the matter through and made the best choice possible under difficult circumstances. For almost all of the mothers I have ever encountered, who were separated from their children by adoption, there was considerable anguish related to the separation. I hope that you can come to understand and empathise with your mother and the many other mothers like her, who felt abandoned by society and pressured into parting with their children, because it was considered to be 'the right thing' to do.

It's been a year now since I was reunited with my mother but sometimes I find that she is insensitive to my feelings and says hurtful things to me. Sometimes I just think I'd be better off not having her in my life. Why can't she be more understanding and think of my feelings more?

Without knowing exactly how your mother has hurt your feelings, it's hard to comment. Have you spoken to her about what it is that you find hurtful? It may be that your mother feels comfortable being honest with you. Only you can judge whether or not she is deliberately trying to upset you, or whether she is unknowingly causing you distress. I hope you can talk to her about this issue and come to some understanding rather than just run away from the relationship because you are finding aspects of it challenging. I'm sure that the relationship could be strengthened by some productive dialogue about areas which are painful for each of you. Hopefully you can discuss maturely how you can both be respectful of the other's feelings, without having to relate to each other in a constrained and uncomfortable manner.

I'm adopted and some people have suggested to me that I could try to find my parents. I think it should be up to them to look for me and so I haven't done anything about it. I presume that they aren't interested as I haven't heard anything from them. What do you think?

I think that you would be doing your parents a great favour by letting them know that you are interested in them and would like to make contact. You can't assume just because you haven't heard from them that they would not like to know about you. They may not be able to get information about you. They may have been trying to find you but not succeeded. They may even have died. If you genuinely want to know your parents, then I suggest that you do everything you can to locate them and then make them an offer of contact. Even if you are unable to find them immediately, you will have a sense of satisfaction from having tried and if you and your parents do get in touch one day, they will know that you cared enough to try to contact them. I am quite sure that my son and I would never have found each other had it not been for the fact that we had both chosen to search.

I really want to develop a relationship with my mother, but sometimes I just don't know how to make conversation with her. I don't want to be always talking about adoption. Have you any suggestions?

Apart from the obvious one of finding out what things she's interested in and how she spends her time and asking her about those things, it's also good to find out which people are important in her life and ask after them too. If your mother has other children who are important to her, that may be hard for you to accept, but it will help if you show that you care about the people that she cares about. If she has a hobby or a lifestyle which makes you uncomfortable or simply bores you, that may be difficult for you too, but it will also help if you show that you are interested in what she does with her time and that you are prepared to accept her as she is and not expect her to change. As time goes on, hopefully it will get easier, as you get to know some of the people in her life, she gets to know some of the people in your life and you also get to share some experiences together. Hopefully she will make some effort too and enquire after the people and events which are important to you.

I was adopted and I also gave up my child for adoption. At the time it just seemed like the right thing to do but now I'm really sad that adoption has affected yet another generation. Is it common for women who were adopted to lose their children through adoption? How can I sort out all the complicated relationships that have been created in my family?

It does happen quite often that women who have been adopted lose custody of their children in one way or another, sometimes through adoption and sometimes more informally. They may also be involved in arranging adoptions, thereby separating other parents from their children. As far as I am aware, there is no research to explain this. It seems that for some, they want somehow to reinforce the idea that adoption was a good thing in their lives and the way to do that is to create yet another adoption situation. Some women seem to think that it will help to reduce the shame and embarrassment they feel about having parents who chose not to raise them, if they then choose not to raise their children also, or support other parents to make this choice. Adopted people are said to lack genealogical continuity. For some women this means that because they have been raised in an adoptive situation, they have not been able to appreciate the value of family relationships. If they have not addressed their own issues in relation to this, they may believe that children are interchangeable and that it makes no difference to them whether or not they are raised in their families. For other women, they lack confidence in their ability to relate to their own child, because they have been raised among people to whom they are not related and they panic at the thought of taking on the responsibilities of parenthood. Some adopted people were raised in abusive environments and feel that they do not have the parenting skills necessary to raise their child. Whatever the reasons, it's a tragedy, but one that can be confronted and dealt with. Your situation is certainly complex, but many people's lives are complex and approaching the situation with honesty and generosity will make it easier for everyone to manage.

I've searched and searched for my mother but have been unable to find her. I know nothing about my father. Will I have to spend the rest of my life in a state of constant anxiety wondering if I'll ever meet them or should I just forget the whole thing and get on with my life?

It's difficult to strike a balance between being aware of the desire to be reunited with your parents, but also being realistic and accepting of the fact that it is not happening at the moment and, like other hopes and dreams, may never happen. It never ceases to amaze me how people do find each other and so I hope that you won't give up hope. However, if you can find a way to incorporate this into your life, then there is no need for your disappointment to prevent you from having a fulfilling life. It might be helpful to practise talking about it in a positive way. For example, if the topic of family comes up in conversation, you could say that you were adopted and that you have tried to locate your family but so far have not been successful. That confirms that it is an important part of your life, but that you are realistic about the difficulties involved. You also never know who might have some useful suggestions for searching that you hadn't thought of before.

My adoptive parents had no idea about raising children and I suffered what I now recognise to be emotional abuse throughout my childhood. I ended up in foster care when I was thirteen. A few years later I was reunited with my parents, who had married and had a happy life without me. They have no other children and are quite well-off. I feel really resentful that they have had such a good life and I had such a rotten life. How can they just expect me to welcome them back into my life when it looks as if I suffered so that they could enjoy life's luxuries?

I'm sure when your parents allowed you to be adopted, they wanted what was best for you. There is no way they could have predicted the kind of life you have had. Do you know why it was that they had no other children? Anecdotal evidence suggests that approximately one third of parents who have been separated from a child through adoption have no further children. I can understand that you are angry, but have you looked closely at who was responsible for your suffering? I'm sure your parents never wanted you to have a miserable life. Your adopters, on the other hand, obviously lacked the skills and compassion needed for their role. It might be helpful for you to learn about the situation your parents were in when they agreed to your adoption, as that may help you to see more clearly where the responsibility lies. The bottom line is that you are now an adult and responsible for your own choices. However, if your parents care about you and are interested in you, then perhaps they could help you to overcome your early disadvantages and have a fulfilling life in spite of them, as many people have done.

I obtained my original birth certificate and after seeing it, I don't think I want to find my parents. There was virtually nothing on it. My mother didn't even give me a name and under 'father' it just says 'not named'. I suppose that means that either she didn't know who had got her pregnant or else he wasn't interested enough to put his name down. Why would I want to meet these people who obviously didn't care anything about me when I was born?

Many mothers were not allowed to name their children. Many fathers were not allowed to be recognised as fathers, simply because they were not married to the child's mother. I think it's unfair of you to make assumptions from this document. My experience shows that original birth certificates do not represent how the parents felt at all, but instead represent how they were excluded from the process and their experiences and their relationship to their child were discounted. I hope that you will be able to contact your parents and hear from them how they really felt. In some places names can be added later to the original birth certificate.

I received a letter from a social worker saying that my mother wants to hear from me. I refused any contact because I don't feel that there's anything missing in my life and I don't feel any need to be in touch with my mother. Do you think that means that there's something wrong with me?

I find your response rather odd. If I called you and invited you to a show would you tell me that you wouldn't go because you don't feel any need to go to a show? If someone invites you somewhere or offers you the opportunity to go somewhere or meet someone, I'm sure it's not because they think that you are somehow lacking because you have not had that experience. Accepting an invitation does not imply that you were already feeling that something was missing. ***Invitations and opportunities are made available to us so that we can choose to enrich our lives and add to our experiences.*** *That doesn't suggest that our lives were not rich before. I don't think you have to feel that something is missing in your life before you can accept an invitation to meet someone. Of course, an invitation to an adoption reunion is much more significant than other invitations in life and so I hope that you'll think about it for a lot longer before you reach a decision. Rather than thinking in terms of what might or might not be missing from your life, maybe you could focus instead on the opportunity that's being offered. Many people in your situation would be overjoyed to receive such a letter.*

I was reunited with my mother recently and we get on well, but I wish she would stop trying to act like a 'mother' to me! I already have one mother who nags me and that's enough. How can I explain this to her without hurting her feelings?

Well, she is your mother, but when we become adults we work out how our relationships with our parents are going to be managed. Each relationship is unique. Of course, the relationship between a parent and an adult child whom they have not raised is different again. All parents respond differently to their children becoming adults and some manage the transition better than others. It sounds as if your mother cares about you and wants to be helpful. I'm sure you can find a sensitive way to acknowledge her intentions, but let her know what it is about her behaviour that makes you uncomfortable. Over time I'm sure you will be able to work co-operatively and create a relationship that suits you.

My mother got in touch with me and I discovered that she had been searching for me for some time. While I appreciate that she was interested in me, when I found out that she had obtained copies of my school photographs and had found out about the births of my children, I felt really invaded. Don't you agree that it's not right for someone to obtain personal information like that about someone they've never even met?

Parents who have been separated from their children by adoption are usually cut off from any knowledge or information about those children and often are desperate to know if their child is still alive, is in good health, has been well-cared for and generally what has become of them. There is no legal barrier to obtaining publicly available information and, for many parents, finding out about their children's lives in this way is their only option to having to live with the agony of never knowing, wondering and worrying. You are right that this effort your mother has made does indicate how much she cares about you and is interested in you. Your mother is not someone whom you have 'never even met'. Your mother and you were intimately connected for nine months and shared the unique experience of your birth together. I hope that you can try to understand what the separation might have meant to her and remember that her actions were well-intentioned. Hopefully you and your mother can go on to build a close relationship and can learn from each other about the time spent apart.

I've been reunited with my parents but they seem to have a hard time accepting me for who I am. My lifestyle is quite different from theirs and I seem to be such a disappointment to them. Why can't they just accept me as I am?

It's very sad that your parents seem to you to be so judgmental and seem to be focussing on your lifestyle rather than the fact that you are their son. Are you able to discuss your feelings with them? Perhaps they don't realise that you sense disappointment in them. It may be that they are not disappointed in you as a person, but that meeting you has forced them to face the fact that they lost the opportunity to raise you. Parents often wonder how their children's lives might have been different if it had not been for the separation. Perhaps you can reassure them that you are happy in your lifestyle and then they might be better able to focus on the positive aspects of your relationship with them.

I have good relationships with both my adoptive parents and my original parents but I find that other people just don't understand. They don't seem to realise how important it is to adopted people to know about their heritage. How can I help them to understand?

The more adoption is brought out into the open and talked about as a part of life, the better others will understand the issues. I know some people are very narrow-minded and just don't want to hear. In cases like that, perhaps you could say something like, 'I'm sorry that you don't seem to understand how I feel. I can appreciate that it must be difficult for you, as you weren't adopted like me. I'd be happy to try to help you to understand.'

I contacted my mother and we spoke once on the telephone. I would really love to exchange letters with her and some day to meet her, but she says that her husband (who is not my father) will not 'allow' her to have any more contact with me. I can't understand how a mature woman could allow her husband to dictate to her in that way. Do you have any suggestions for me?

Sadly, many mothers were bullied into giving up their children and, as a result, submitting to bullying became a habit for them. Some mothers have been able to understand what happened to them and have used their experience to make sure that they are no longer submissive and compliant as they were when they lost their children. Others, however, have not gained strength from their loss, but rather have gone through their lives as victims. I would suggest that you tell your mother that you care about her and will continue to contact her regularly, but perhaps not frequently for now. Hopefully your messages will finally lead her to gain the confidence and courage she needs, to refuse to tolerate her husband's bullying and to accept your generous offer of reunion.

My mother died when I was ten years old. My father later remarried and I was adopted by my stepmother. They eventually divorced but then I was horrified, when I was planning my marriage, to be told that my original birth certificate with my mother's name on it was no longer a legal document and that I would have to record my stepmother's name as my mother. I knew and loved my mother and I haven't seen my stepmother for years. I had no idea that being adopted by her would mean that for the rest of my life I would have to deny my dear mother. Can I have the adoption reversed?

In most places it's not legally possible to have an adoption rescinded, but I suggest that you seek legal advice in the area in which you were adopted. These days stepparent adoptions are practically non-existent in Australia and your case is a very good reason why they are being phased out. There was absolutely no justification for your adoption and I'm very sorry that this has happened to you. I hope that you will be able to take legal steps to rectify the situation.

Although I've always known that I was adopted, I was never interested in trying to find my relatives. In fact, I had no idea that I even had another birth certificate until I read your book. Then I made enquiries and was able to obtain a copy of my original birth certificate, which had my original name on it and my mother's name. I was just amazed at how deeply that affected me. I was suddenly confronted with the reality that I existed as a person before my adoption. I felt as if the rug had been pulled from under me. I've been really emotional ever since, but now I just feel paralysed and don't think I can take the next step. What would you advise?

I'm very glad that you have started to explore your identity and your origins. I don't believe that having your birth certificate has caused you to be upset, but rather that it has triggered the emotions which have been buried deeply inside, since you were separated from your families of origin. Many adopted people say that their adoption had never been an issue for them, when what they mean is, that they had buried their feelings and chosen not to explore its implications in their lives. I think the first thing is for you to accept your feelings and understand that they are appropriate. Once you feel that you have begun to accommodate your grief, then you will have the confidence to proceed, knowing that you will benefit from knowing the truth, no matter what the outcome. It's important that you go at your own pace and be prepared to accept whatever you find with equanimity. You're on an exciting journey, unlike anything you have ever experienced. Whatever happens, it will be a tremendous growing and learning experience for you.

I can't understand why so many women just gave away their babies in the 1960s and 1970s. How could they have done that?

In those days there was a lot of shame and guilt attached to an out-of-wedlock pregnancy. Reputation was very important then. Young women were valued very much on the basis of their sexual reputations and the whole family could be judged on the basis of the behaviour of one member. In many cases, the parents of the mother could not tolerate an illegitimate grandchild, as this was considered by many to bring shame on the whole family. Illegitimate children also carried the shame and guilt from their parents. They were sometimes stigmatised and, in some circles, considered inferior. At one time, for example, anyone who was illegitimate was barred from entering university (this actually happened to Leonardo Da Vinci). Once, illegitimate children could not even inherit from their mothers, never mind their fathers, because an illegitimate child was considered to be 'the child of no one'. Parents were told that allowing their child to grow up illegitimate would constitute a very real disadvantage for the child. Also many mothers were not supported by the fathers of their children and if they also did not have support from their parents, they had no way of providing financially either for themselves or for a child. There were no government benefits then to support single parent families as single parenthood was considered undesirable and therefore to be discouraged, not encouraged. It was almost impossible in most places for single mothers to find accommodation or employment. Mothers were frequently told that it would be selfish of them to try to raise their children if they were not married and that they should put their children's welfare first and give them the opportunities in life that a married couple could provide. Some of these attitudes persisted long after the 1970s. It might be helpful for you to read some of the work produced by mothers and fathers, describing their experiences.

My mother says that she never actually had sexual intercourse with my father. Surely she must be wrong?

I've heard of cases where a pregnancy has resulted from sexual behaviour which apparently stopped short of actual intercourse. It's certainly possible and, in the social climate in which your parents were growing up, not unheard of at all. For previous generations, the attitude to sexual behaviour before marriage was not open and accepting as it is in many societies now. Young people were expected to refrain from sexual intercourse until they were married and that is why there was such a degree of shame attached to an out-of-wedlock pregnancy. Such sexual behaviour as did occur was generally rather frantic and furtive. You have to remember also that, at that time, there was no sex education in schools and that most young people were very naïve when it came to the mechanics of sexual intercourse. Contraceptives were not readily available, nor was information. In many cases there was uncertainty about whether or not actual intercourse had occurred and, for many young women, who did not believe that they had participated in a completed act of intercourse, the pregnancy came as an enormous shock.

When I hear you talk about bringing about an end to adoption, it makes me feel that adoption is something awful and then I feel awful because I was adopted. Is adoption really such a bad thing?

Saying that there should be no more adoptions certainly does not mean that there is anything wrong with being adopted. I hope that I have made the distinction clear. I would not want to be adding to the shame that has already permeated so many people's adoption experiences. I have never heard of an adoption taking place for vindictive or cruel reasons. However, in spite of the motives of those involved, a great deal of suffering has been caused. What I am saying is that we should learn from the experiences and the sufferings of those who have already been involved in adoptions and use that knowledge to create more effective and humane responses to life's difficulties.

I'm adopted and my father has sent me a letter. I didn't think he had the right to do that. Does he?

As far as I know there is no law that prevents a person from writing a letter to another person. I assume that his letter is not threatening or abusive in any way. If your father has written to you, then that suggests that he cares about you and is interested in you. As far as I'm aware, it's neither illegal nor morally wrong to care enough to write someone a letter. I hope that you'll appreciate his effort and respond warmly to him. There are many adopted people who would be delighted to receive such a letter.

It's been wonderful to meet my mother again, but it seems to me that for her, meeting me brings back all her hurt and sadness from the time I was born. I feel guilty that I was the cause of such pain. It's hard to enjoy being with her when I can see the hurt in her eyes, especially if I talk about my childhood or my adoptive family. Will she ever get over this and be able to enjoy spending time with me?

Your mother is working through her grief but it sounds as if she could benefit from some assistance. Perhaps you could suggest to her that she find a way to explore her grief and work through it in a way that will not impinge on her relationship with you. It will be difficult for her to hear about the life which you led without her. Perhaps she is not quite ready for that yet. Be patient with her, as grief does go through stages and her pain will not necessarily always be so obviously present when you are together.

My mother has made contact with me through an agency but I feel that I'm happy in my life and don't want to disrupt it by allowing her to intrude. Shouldn't the social worker involved be validating my feelings instead of trying to persuade me to respond to my mother?

It's not the social worker's job to try to persuade you to do anything, but to support you to explore your options and to act in what you believe to be your best interests. I think you have confused validation of your feelings with support for your actions. For example, if a mother comes to me and tells me that she is very sad because she has lost a child through adoption, then I will tell her that her feelings of grief are natural and productive and will hopefully lead to a positive outcome ie the processing of her grief and the incorporation of the grief into her life. In that way, I would validate her feelings. However, if she said that she found the grieving process too difficult and was planning to end her life rather than deal with it, I would not support her in taking such action. Adopters might approach me and say that they had been contacted on behalf of the mother of their adopted daughter, but that they did not want to tell the adopted child, as they were afraid of the outcome. While I would validate their feelings of concern for their adopted daughter, I could not support the way in which they wished to express that concern. I would talk to them about their love for their adopted child and how they could express that love in a generous, caring way, which would allow their adopted daughter to exercise her own decision-making powers. You may not have explored the impact of adoption separation in your life. If I were your social worker, I would validate your feelings of fear and anxiety, but I would also want to try to encourage you to examine what has happened in your life, explore the possibilities for the future with you and to talk about what might be in your best interests.

I met my mother but afterwards I wished that I hadn't. She takes drugs, she has no job and she just seems to have drifted through life and not achieved anything. It just seemed that we have nothing at all in common. So after meeting her once I told her that

I wasn't interested in seeing her again. I was so disappointed and so I just felt that there was no point. She's upset and says I should never have searched for her if I was just going to disappear out of her life again. Do you think she's right?

It's not uncommon for family members who have been separated by adoption to find that they have taken quite different journeys through life and that they do not share the same values. However this also happens in families where there has been no adoption separation experience. Your mother is your mother regardless of the circumstances which she has had to face in her life and the ways in which she has chosen to deal with those circumstances. ***Your mother is not responsible for your disappointment.*** *If you had certain expectations of her, which she has not met, then you are responsible for that, not your mother. You may have felt when you searched for your mother that you wanted to have her in your life forever, but no one can predict what they will experience after the reunion has occurred. I hope that you will think about this a bit more and find a way to accept your differences and be able to acknowledge and nurture your relationship.*

I'm adopted and since being reunited with my parents, I always seem to feel that it's my job to keep everyone happy. I frantically try to juggle time spent with both sets of parents so that I don't upset any of them. Will it always be this difficult?

Many adopted people seem to feel responsible for the feelings of others. Perhaps it would be helpful to you to read about the impact of adoption on the lives of those who are adopted and that might help you to understand better why you feel the way you do. You are not responsible for the feelings of others. All of your parents are adults and they are responsible for their own feelings. They all have to learn to deal with the impact of adoption on their lives. I suggest that you just relax and enjoy your time with them.

When I was reunited with my mother, I told her that I had had a good upbringing and that I was grateful for having been adopted. Isn't that what mothers want to hear?

I find it very distressing (and I know that many parents do) to hear adopted people say that they are 'glad' that they were adopted or that they are 'grateful' for having been adopted. For many mothers this is a cruel, hurtful thing to hear. It often translates to mothers as, 'I'm so glad I wasn't raised by ***you*** *– how awful would that have been?' No one could ever know what might have happened if the adoption had not taken place and so it is not only not helpful, but also can be very damaging for someone to assume that their life would have been unhappier had they not been adopted. Life is by its nature unpredictable and complex. Imagine, if you can, that you are a parent and that one of your children tells you that they wished that someone else had raised them and had acted as a parent to them instead of you. Can you imagine how hurtful that could be? I sometimes hear adopted people say that if they hadn't been adopted they would have had a poor and unhappy childhood. No one knows that. No one can ever know what might have happened. They may not have been poor – and besides, being poor does not necessarily mean being unhappy, any more than being rich guarantees happiness. Many poor people have a very rich emotional life, while many rich people are miserable. Being young and poor is not a permanent condition and having a young, poor parent is also not necessarily a harmful environment for children. There are much worse situations. Being adopted is not something to be glad or grateful about. It is an unchangeable part of your history, which you have to learn to accept. It is tragic that there are so many people who seem to feel that they have to justify adoption by insisting that children who were adopted were 'better off' than they would have been if they had been raised by either their mothers or their fathers. Every child has issues to deal with in their family, but for adopted children there are the added complications of being* *raised among people to whom they are not related and the fact that the community sometimes regards them with distrust or distaste because of their unknown origins. It is impossible to say that adopted children have fared better in their adoptive families than they would have done being raised by their mother and/or father, as there is no way of knowing what might have been. No one knows and no one is in a position to assume, what life might have been like for those children. If, at the time of the pregnancy, those parents had been encouraged to think in terms of family preservation, of their parental roles and their value to their children, their lives may have taken a very different direction. They may have taken their parental responsibilities seriously and found supportive people who recognised the significance of their relationship with their children. In some cases, the parents of the child would have stayed together and the child would have been raised by two people to whom they were related and thus avoided the emotional complications of being raised in an adoptive home. Even if those children had been raised by only one parent, there are other people in children's lives who share in their development and are important to them, to whom they may or may not be related. A life with one loving, dedicated parent is not by any means a barren life. There may have been unpleasant attitudes in the community towards a child who was not living with two parents who were married to each other, but perhaps adversity rather than privilege would have helped them to develop different qualities eg compassion and courage. Also you never know how your parents' lives would have been had they not lost their child. They also may have developed different qualities eg determination and independence. Being a single parent encouraged me to provide security for my children; I bought a home, I returned to study and took up different careers. Adversity can give us the opportunity to develop coping strategies and to access our inner strengths in a way that comfort does not.*

I was always quite content with the fact that I was adopted. I felt that I accepted it and didn't let it affect me very much. I was never interested in looking for my parents, but then I got a telephone call from my father. When I realised who it was, I burst into tears and cried for days afterwards. I couldn't decide if I was happy or sad. Why do you think it affected me that way?

I think that you actually had deep feelings of grief created by the separation from your parents, although it seems that you did not recognise those feelings until your father's call triggered them. It sounds as if his contact brought to the surface a deep sense of loss and sadness for you that you had buried without being aware of it. I'm delighted for you that your father has contacted you and that you have been given the opportunity to acknowledge your grief. I hope that you will go on to explore and express your feelings as you build relationships with your family members.

Why do some mothers and fathers object to being called 'birthparents' (or 'birth parents')?

Many people are concerned about the use of terms such as these. Some parents feel that if they are referred to as the 'birthparents' (or 'birth parents') then that suggests that they are not actual parents, but only the parents who caused the birth to happen. For some, it implies that they were simply 'breeders'. Using that term can seem to suggest that after the birth they were no longer parents and that they have a lower status than the adopters. Many parents find the term insulting and demeaning. I know that there are some, however, who do not. The key point is that you discuss with your parents how they prefer to be named and that you are able to reach an agreement on the matter.

It's not my fault I was adopted. My parents abandoned me when I was a baby and gave me up for adoption. How can I ever forgive them for that?

I don't think it's helpful to talk about adoption in terms of fault. Were your adopters at fault for wanting a child so much, that they were prepared to take someone else's and pretend it was theirs? Were your parents at fault for wanting you to have the advantages they thought they couldn't give you? Was the system at fault for allowing children to be adopted and causing so much misery and confusion? Was society at fault for not supporting family preservation and instead removing children from their families? I really don't think that trying to apportion blame is going to be helpful to anyone. In my experience it only encourages bitterness, which can be very destructive. Personally, I don't use the word 'forgive' as it has connotations of sin and guilt, which I don't find helpful. Every parent I have ever met, who has lost a child through adoption, had been told that their child would benefit from being adopted. It is difficult to understand, therefore, how some adopted people consider that allowing them to be adopted was some kind of 'sin' on the part of the parents, for which the adopted adult may or may not choose to forgive them. Cases in which children were truly 'abandoned' are very rare. For most parents they had no notion of abandoning their children at all. If the adopted adult feels that they did not, in fact, benefit in any way from being adopted, then why should their parents be held responsible for this? If the adopters did not provide the child with a supportive and fulfilling home atmosphere in which to grow up, then whose responsibility is that? People act in line with their beliefs. Parents were led to believe that there were circumstances in their lives which would be detrimental to their children's growth and development and that adopters would not find themselves in such circumstances. Parents who were unmarried were also told that their children would suffer from the stigma of being labelled as illegitimate. Do you really think it's about forgiving?

My mother and I have been reunited but we don't feel like mother and daughter. I don't think of her as my mother and we feel more like friends. Is that normal?

You are mother and daughter, regardless of whether or not you 'feel like' mother and daughter. There is no set pattern for how a mother and daughter feel about each other. Some mothers and daughters hate each other and some mothers and daughters love each other. It's about acknowledging who you are. You are a daughter and a mother. You are most definitely not 'friends'. How you feel about each other doesn't have to be compared with how other people feel about each other. You don't ask a husband and wife if they 'feel like' husband and wife. They are husband and wife regardless of how they feel. Some husbands and wives love each other and some hate each other. What you are (ie mother and child, or brother and sister) is a quite separate issue from how you feel. Once you openly acknowledge who you are, then you can begin to relate to each other and to build a relationship. Your relationship doesn't have to conform to any sort of model. It doesn't have to be like the relationship of any other mother and daughter (each one is unique). It's your relationship and it's up to both of you to shape it. Pretending that the relationship does not exist, however, is dishonest and unproductive. It's not how you feel about someone that defines your relationship with that person. The relationship exists regardless of your feelings, not because of your feelings. If you are an adopted person and you meet the woman who gave birth to you, you have not met a friend, you have met your mother. If your mother died in childbirth and you never knew her or if you are separated from her shortly after your birth and you grow up not knowing her, that does not alter her relationship to you. Some people have close relationships with their mothers; some do not. Some people have no interaction with their mothers at all. The quality of the interaction does not define the nature of the relationship. Acknowledging who our family members are, however, is an important factor in defining who we are and where we fit in the world.

I've been reunited with my mother and I've discovered that she has very little education and has spent her life working in unskilled jobs. I was raised in a family which places a high value on education and all the members of my adoptive family have professional qualifications. I find it difficult to communicate with my mother because of her low level of education. Do you have any suggestions?

She is your mother, no matter what her level of education. It might help to foster the relationship if you are able to emphasise the similarities between you and your mother and not place too much stress on the differences. Your mother does not have to earn her place in your life, no matter what path her life has taken. Hopefully you can reassure her that your feelings for her are not dependent on her achievements, but that you care for her because you are her daughter. I'm sure that she has many admirable qualities which are not taught in institutions of higher learning. If you are able to approach the relationship with sensitivity and compassion then I'm sure that the differences between you do not need to have a negative impact on your future together.

I've received a letter saying that my mother wants to hear from me. She had her chance to have me as part of her family when I was a baby and she didn't want me then. She didn't care about me when I was born and now she's trying to come back into my life. Why should I want to meet her now?

If you think that allowing you to be adopted shows that your mother didn't care about you, then I think that you are probably wrong. Most mothers were told that if they cared anything for their children, they would agree for them to be adopted. I know from talking to many mothers and fathers, that they have never stopped caring about their children over the years. There is a sense in which your mother has always been in your life, in the same way that all parents live on in their children. I'm sure that it must make you feel good to know that your mother is still concerned about you and I'm sure she always has been. For most parents, it wasn't about whether or not they 'wanted' their children, it was about wanting what was best for their children. Your mother was probably told that the way to prove that she was concerned about you was to have you adopted. That's what most young, unmarried parents were told many years ago. They were often told that they should sacrifice what they wanted, in order to do what was best for their children. They probably also hoped that their children would understand what their motives were in allowing them to be adopted. I'm sure your mother wanted the best in life for you and didn't think that she could give you that. It's great that she wants to hear from you now. I hope that you'll be able to meet up with her soon and that you can hear from her exactly what happened, how she felt then and how she feels now, rather than continue making unfounded assumptions.

I'm adopted and I'm confused about who my 'relatives' are. Are they members of my adoptive family or members of my original families or all of them?

Adoption creates a close legal relationship, in a similar way to what a marriage does. Sometimes this results in a close emotional relationship. Sometimes it does not. However, being legally connected to someone, either through marriage or through adoption, does not mean that one is related to that person. A husband and wife have a legal relationship, for example, but they do not share the same genes. Having a blood relationship does not, of itself, necessarily create an emotional closeness any more than having a legal relationship does. However, there is a distinction between those to whom we are related by blood and those to whom we are related by a legal connection such as marriage or adoption.

A woman came to my door claiming to be my mother. She's the woman who gave birth to me but as far as I'm concerned that doesn't make her my mother. I've had a very happy upbringing and am quite content with my life as it is. I have a mother and I'm not looking for another one. How dare this woman intrude in my life like that? How can I make sure that I never hear from her again?

In fact, she is your mother, whether or not you choose to acknowledge that fact. Sometimes people know the truth but choose to push it to the back of their minds in order to avoid addressing it. There's a lot of denial connected with adoption relationships and a lot of hostility related to reunion events. Your mother appears to have taken you by surprise and approached you when you did not feel ready for reunion. ***However, your mother is not responsible for the fact that you were not prepared for the reunion****. In fact, she has always been your mother. Perhaps now that she has come back into your life, you could consider your options more carefully. You could perhaps appreciate the opportunity which your mother has given you and use the occasion to think about exploring the impact of adoption on your life. I hope that you can learn how to express your anger in a productive way, to work through your grief and confront reality, to accept your mother's offer of contact graciously and to find it in your heart to include her in your life again.*

I felt after reading your book that I finally had some understanding of what it might have been like for my mother to have given me up. However, when I eventually met her, she was very cool about it all and said that the pregnancy had come at an inconvenient time, when she wanted to pursue her career. She doesn't seem to have suffered much from having been separated from me, which is quite disappointing. Is it just not such a big deal for some mothers?

It's impossible to generalise about adoption outcomes as there are so many variables. I believe that most parents suffer deeply from the loss of their children, but I have met some who seem to have been able to process their feelings at the time of the loss and so, in later years, perhaps at the time of reunion, they seem to be less affected emotionally. There are others, however, who have been very successful at shutting down their emotions and denying their feelings. For those mothers, even when a reunion takes place, they are still not willing to get in touch with their buried feelings, because they fear being overwhelmed by the pain. I cannot guess what might be happening for your mother, but I do know that I have never met a mother who lost a child through adoption who was not deeply affected by the separation.

My mother refuses to tell me who my father is. My father and his family are my relatives too and I want to know about them. Is there anything I can do if my mother refuses to help me?

It's very sad that your mother has chosen not to support you in seeking your father. Hopefully she will come to realise that you are a product of two parents and that it is in your best interests to have knowledge and understanding about both of your families of origin. It may be that your mother has not addressed her own issues regarding her relationship with your father. If she continues to refuse to assist you, there may be documents relating to the adoption which might provide you with information, or there may be other family members who know of your father. I hope you won't give up, as there are many potential benefits, for all three of you (you, your mother and your father) in confronting the events of the past and in exploring possible relationships for the future. Perhaps you could try to talk to your mother about this again and hope that she will come to see these benefits.

I'm 55 years old and I found out when my adoptive parents died that I was adopted. I feel very angry that I was deceived all my life. Is it too late for me to find out who I am and who my relatives are?

It's never too late and although it's sad that you have been deceived for so long, at least you have the opportunity now to begin the search for your families. I would advise that you don't wait any longer.

My father tried to contact me through a social worker and instead of contacting me directly, the social worker contacted my adoptive parents. I'm an adult. How dare she do that? Surely that's unethical?

I agree with you completely, that this was unethical behaviour and, as a social worker, I would never consider acting in that way. I've been told by social workers in the United Kingdom that they fear being sued by adopters for breaching their confidentiality by telling their adult adopted children that they are adopted and that this is the reason that they contact adopters. Some social workers, however, take it further and seek permission from the adopters, before they will proceed to contact the adult adopted person. I find their stance totally insupportable and unprofessional. As an adult, you are able to vote, apply for a firearms licence, go to war for your country, drive a car, get married and become a parent, among other things, yet it seems that your confidentiality has not been respected with regard to being in touch with your family members and you have not been allowed to make an adult decision. It's no wonder that some adopted people complain of being treated like eternal children by those in authority. You might want to consider a formal complaint or even legal action. Social workers need to know that this appalling behaviour will no longer be tolerated.

I'm adopted. That means that my parents rejected me when I was born. Why should I let them into my life now? What if they reject me again?

When your parents lost the right to raise you, it was not because of any individual traits or qualities that you possessed. They probably knew little, if anything, about you. They may not even have seen you. Because they had to make a decision about the implications of the family and social situation in which they found themselves and to try to predict how it would affect both you and them, that doesn't mean that they rejected you. It was not a personal decision, in that they did not regard you personally as in any way an undesirable child. You may have felt rejected but that is a feeling, not a fact. I have never yet heard a mother or father say that in allowing their child to be adopted, they were rejecting or abandoning that child. Such terminology can be very hurtful to parents and I wish that more people could understand that. For those adopted people who believe that, as a baby, they were somehow not good enough for their parents and were therefore given away, it can be helpful to look at themselves as they are and to realise that their parents had no way of knowing what that baby would become. If your parents now refuse contact with you, that doesn't mean that they will be rejecting you either. In fact, I have never heard anyone say that in refusing contact they are 'rejecting' the other party. It could mean that they are not willing to confront the truth and deal with their grief issues at this time in their lives. If they know nothing about you, they can't reject you personally. It may feel like a rejection, but, in fact, it would be a refusal on their behalf to face the truth and the implications of the past. Adopted people who are considering reunion may want to think about what there is about what they have become, that their parents may appreciate and enjoy. Making contact with your parents is a risk, of course. It takes courage. You have no way of knowing whether or not they are ready for such a contact, but hopefully you will be able to overcome your fear and offer them that opportunity.

I'm so amazed at how much my health has improved since I was reunited with my parents. I used to suffer from a variety of health issues, some of which the medical profession could not explain. Now I feel so much better. I know some adopted people say that they search to get medical information but have you heard of people whose health has improved after reunion even without receiving any medical information?

Yes, I certainly have. For many adopted people and their parents, the separation and the reactions to the loss have caused a range of health problems. The stress related to burying the grief has also been a factor. In many cases, being able to confront the reality of the separation and grieve the loss brings relief from those problems and a noticeable improvement in overall well-being.

I've been thinking about trying to trace my origins but I want to make it clear that I'm not looking for a mother as I already have a mother. I would really just like some medical information from the woman who gave birth to me. I think she owes it to me to provide that. Don't you agree?

First of all, if you find the woman who gave birth to you, you will have found your mother. Some people have more than one person in their life who fills a maternal role. If you do find her and she is still alive, you will have found a living, breathing, feeling person, not just a provider of information. In fact, your mother does not owe you anything. I think it would be wise for you to try to prepare yourself a bit more for the implications of searching for your mother before you go any further with your plans and to remember that no one can predict what they will experience after the reunion has occurred.

I've often wondered about the families from which I came, but my adoptive parents have been so good to me. Do you think it would be disloyal to them if I try to contact my original parents?

Many adopters are delighted when their adopted children try to find out about their families, as they see it as a sign that they have raised them to accept themselves as being made up of a combination of their heritage and their environment. Unconditional love doesn't demand a type of loyalty which would prevent growth and personal fulfilment. Genuine (ie unconditional and generous) love will not be eroded by the truth. If your adopters love you, I'm sure they would not want you to be denied this very important opportunity.

I didn't find out that I was adopted until after my adoptive parents died. I'm so glad that I did find out as it helped to explain a lot of things for me and allowed me finally to get to know my families. Can you explain why anyone could have thought it was morally acceptable to lie to me for all those years?

It's difficult to apply the views of today to the decisions made in the past. Many adopters thought that they were protecting their children from the pain that the knowledge of their adoption might bring. Others did not want to face the truth for reasons of their own. Since your adopters are now deceased, I hope that you can work through your outrage and disappointment and focus on their motives and not their ignorance. It will also help for you to consider the positive experiences which you have had in your life and how you have made the most of your opportunities.

I met up with my mother a few years ago and it was a great reunion but after a couple of years the relationship just seemed to die a natural death. It seems that her curiosity has been satisfied and that she has lost interest in me. Should I just leave things as they are?

Many people come and go in our lives. Some people enter our lives and remain there until one of us dies; other people are in our lives for a period of time and then we drift apart. A relationship usually will only continue to thrive if both parties want the relationship enough to put some effort into it. Sometimes misunderstandings arise and assumptions are made. Your mother may also be dealing with other issues in her life at this time, of which you are unaware. It might be a good idea to let your mother know that you still care for her and that you are still willing to maintain some kind of contact, even if it's only an occasional card or letter to catch up. It wouldn't take much effort and she may be delighted to know that you still care. On the other hand, if she has no interest in maintaining a relationship, at least you might find that out and can stop wondering.

I've thought about trying to find my parents, but I've heard that most adoption reunions don't work out and I'm afraid of being hurt. Should I take the risk of opening up a can of worms or just let sleeping dogs lie?

I have never understood why people talk about adoption reunions in terms of whether or not they 'work out'. When someone is raised within the family to which they were born, I never hear them say that their relationships with family members 'didn't work out', in spite of the fact that, when they are adults, they have good relationships with some family members but not with others. If a mother and child do not have a close relationship, regardless of whether or not they have spent the child's developing years together, does that mean that that particular mother/child relationship did not 'work out'? Or does it mean that mother/child relationships, in general, do not 'work out'? Some mothers and their adult children have close relationships and some do not. Most adults have close relationships with their parents and most adults also have close relationships with people other than their parents. Many adopted adults have close relationships in both their families of origin and their adoptive families. They do not necessarily have equally close relationships with all family members, any more than do adults who are raised in their families of origin. As for opening up a 'can of worms' – I'm a mother who was separated from my child by adoption and for me it is very distasteful and offensive to be referred to in such terms. Of course, seeking out your families of origin is a step into the unknown and takes courage. Sadly, there are those who allow their fear to prevent a reunion from taking place. Too often fear overrides generosity of spirit and holds a person back from reaching out and meeting a family member from whom they have been separated by adoption. My son and I were reunited only because we both overcame our fears and we both felt courageous and generous enough to search for each other. I feel that it is part of my role to help people to overcome their fears. If they can first of all understand what it is that is happening to them, they will already be less fearful. If they can then replace some of their fear with generosity, both to themselves and to the other party, then they may come to a point of being able to meet. If I can show people that there is much to be gained for both parties to the reunion and that fear is preventing them from having growing experiences, which will enrich and deepen their lives, then they often feel more inclined to proceed towards reunion.

I would really like my parents and my adoptive parents to get on well together as they are all important to me. They have never met but my birthday is coming up and I was thinking about inviting all of them so that they could meet. I just want to be part of one big, happy family. Do you think this is a good idea?

First of all, for adopted people (and their parents) their birthday is often an occasion of mixed emotions and so your birthday party is probably not a good choice for this sort of meeting. While you may want your parents and your adopters to like each other, this may not happen. I think it would be better if you leave it up to them to decide if and when they want to meet. Perhaps you could just emphasise to them how important they are to you and let them decide if and when they want to share time together.

I've thought about trying to find my parents, but some people are telling me that it would be selfish of me to contact them. I don't want to ruin their lives by bringing up the past for them. Do I have the right to do that?

Every mother who has lost a child through adoption knows that she has had a child. Many fathers who have lost children through adoption also know that they have fathered a child. All of these mothers and fathers know that there is a possibility that there will be a reunion with that child one day. Some have chosen to anticipate and prepare themselves for the possibility of that event and some have not. There are, of course, cases where the parents were led to believe that the child had died and there are fathers who were never told about the pregnancy. These parents have had no opportunity to prepare themselves. You have no way of knowing how ready your parents might be to meet you again, but you will be doing them a great favour by giving them that opportunity. In my view, it's not about rights, it's about opportunities. I don't think that making contact with your parents would be selfish. In fact I believe it is a very generous act.

I was so happy to find my mother and my father. They are both really nice people and I get on well with them. My adoptive parents are also very nice people and I had a really happy childhood. I've read a lot about the loss and grief associated with adoption but I just don't seem to feel that way. Am I missing something?

Well, every loss situation is unique and everyone responds to loss in their own way. For some people their sense of loss after an adoption separation is less intense than it is for others. I wouldn't go looking for pain if it doesn't seem to be there. I'm very glad that you were able to recognise that growing up adopted is different from growing up with the families into which you were born and that you were open to meeting your families. Your parents, however, may not have escaped from the experience unscathed and you may also have grief which is yet to surface. I'm very glad to hear that you have good relationships with all your various family connections and it's good to see that you can accept that all of them have their place. Enjoy!

I've recently met my mother and overall I believe that it has been a great experience for me. However, sometimes I just seem to fly off the handle with her and then I feel bad about it afterwards. I don't really understand why this happens. Is this normal?

It's certainly all right to be angry about the impact of adoption separation in your life, but, in my opinion, it's not healthy or productive to express that anger towards your mother. I feel that that kind of behaviour can only be destructive to a relationship which, at this stage, needs to be nurtured, not challenged. Too often the anger which is part of the grieving process is translated into name-calling and blaming. In my opinion, this kind of abusive behaviour is to be avoided at all costs. I hope that you will find ways to explore and express your anger which are productive and healthy, as this will actually help to foster a close relationship with your mother, rather than alienating her with unkind and hurtful words.

I rang my mother and introduced myself and she said that she hates me. How can she hate me when she has never met me?

It's interesting that she expresses such strong feelings towards you. At least she's clearly not indifferent to you! Adoption reunion situations tend to rekindle feelings of loss and grief related to the original separation. Hostility is a common component of grieving behaviour. What she hates at the moment, I suspect, is not you as a person, but the idea that you exist. She may hate and fear her history and her pain associated with that history. Fear of the truth and the impact of the truth on people's lives sometimes holds them back from getting involved in a reunion. It is very sad that people choose to live with lies and fear instead of openness and honesty. Hopefully she will not allow her current fear to prevent her from considering your generous offer of contact. I suggest that you allow her some time to consider and then make your offer again, perhaps by letter, which is less confronting. Hopefully, one day soon, she will recognise the depth of her feelings, decide to address them and feel ready to accept your offer graciously.

I now realise when I look back at my childhood that my adoptive mother was quite mentally and emotionally unbalanced. Is that common?

Yes, it is. There are many possible explanations for why this is the case. It would be interesting for some research to be conducted on the mental health issues of adopters.

I'm considering trying to find my parents but I'm worried about how that might affect my adoptive parents. How do adoptive parents generally feel when their adopted children meet up with their parents or other family members?

If you are a parent, you are aware as you are raising your children that when they are adults they will form their own relationships. If you have chosen to raise someone else's children (ie adopted children) then you will be aware that this may also include forming relationships with members of their families of origin. Many adopters see these relationships as a positive and desirable stage of their adopted child's adult development. This could also be an opportunity for growth and learning for all concerned.

Chapter 3
Questions asked by others

Questions asked by adopters

Why don't you talk about the way adoptive parents experience reunion?

Adoption reunions are about reuniting family members who have been separated from each other by adoption. Adopters do not experience reunions because they have never been separated from a family member by adoption. Therefore I do not discuss what the experience of reunion may mean to adopters as they are not participants in the reunion. They are observers, supporters and interested others, but the reunion is never their experience. If you wanted to know, for example, what it feels like to get married, you would ask the bride and groom, not the best man. Sometimes adopters believe that the reunion experience should be theirs and their attempts to be involved have been known to create unnecessary complications for the adult adopted person. Emotional support from the adopters, on the other hand, can be very valuable.

I may be an adoptive mother but I'm the only mother my adopted daughter has ever known. Why should I be cast aside just because her original mother has decided to come into her life after I was the one who did all the work to raise her?

Sadly, adopters sometimes complain that they feel as if they have been only 'temporary care-givers' who are then 'cast aside' when the 'real' parents come back into their adopted child's life. The role of any parent is to be a temporary care-giver – to care for children until those children become adults and are able to care for themselves. The only parents whose care-giving role continues past the age of adulthood of their children are parents whose children have a disability which prevents them from taking full responsibility for their own care. In cases where no such disability exists, if we raise our children effectively, then we expect that our care will no longer be required when they become adults. In healthy, secure relationships between adopters and their adopted children, an adult child's relationship with their families of origin is not viewed as a threat to the relationship between the adopters and the adult adopted child.

I'm an adoptive parent and our adopted son has no interest in finding his original families. I'm disappointed and feel as if we've failed him. Where did we go wrong?

I can understand your disappointment, but you are not responsible for the decisions he makes. You can reassure him that you feel that it would be in his best interests to seek out his families and that you will be happy to support him in this. However, he needs to do this when he feels ready. Confronting the truth about the place of adoption separation in our lives requires a degree of courage. Seeking a reunion requires a spirit of generosity. People will only draw on those qualities and act on them when they have sufficient understanding of the meaning of their adoption experience in their lives and when they are able to overcome any anxiety they may feel about confronting the truth.

Our adopted daughter searched for her original parents and met them and we weren't allowed to share this experience with her because she did it all behind our backs. We were very hurt by her actions. Wouldn't it have been better for her to be open and honest about what she was doing?

When our children become adults, there are many parts of their lives which they choose not to share with their parents. I'm sure that there are aspects of your lives that you have chosen not to share with your parents. This is generally considered to be quite appropriate. Sometimes adopted adults do not include their adopters in their reunion plans because they fear their disapproval or because they fear their interference. Sometimes, however, it's just that they feel the need to experience reunion alone without outside influences. It's their experience and they need to feel a sense of ownership of what's happening and to feel confident that they are managing it in their own way. If you had a healthy relationship with your daughter before her reunion, then it's unlikely that this will be adversely affected by her having contact with her parents. In fact, the opposite is usually the case. After reunion, adopted adults usually feel more comfortable with themselves and therefore are better able to relate to other people. However, for many people the reunion is an emotional trauma and it can take time for those emotions to settle. It would be helpful for your adopted daughter if you can try to understand her experience and support her through it.

When we adopted our daughter we thought that we were doing a good thing, but, now that I understand about the outcomes of adoption, I'm sorry that I was a part of a system which caused so much pain. I feel that I want to apologise to my daughter for the mistake I made in adopting her. Do you think she'll forgive me?

It's great that you understand that there was no need for the adoption to have taken place, but I don't think you should blame yourself. I'm sure that you wanted what was best for your adopted daughter and that you didn't know any better at the time. I don't think it's about forgiving; I think it's more valuable to consider the adoption in its historical and social context and to focus on your motives and intentions.

We never lied about the fact that our children were adopted, but we didn't think it was necessary for the children to be constantly reminded of it. In what ways do you find that adoptive parents fail to acknowledge the truth about their adopted children's origins?

Sometimes this happens by default, for example, failing to correct others when they assume that the children have inherited certain characteristics or will inherit certain characteristics from their adopters. This can, in fact, be an opportunity to state the truth and show the child that there is no shame attached to the fact that they are not related by blood to their adopters. I met one adopter, for example, who introduced me to his adopted son with the comment that the son clearly took 'his good looks from his mother' (referring to the adoptive mother). Deliberately stating such untruths with regard to an adopted child can give the message to the child that their adopted status is something shameful and must be concealed. This is not likely to foster a good self-image in the child.

I'm afraid that if my adopted son finds out the truth about his origins, that it will ruin his life. Surely, in some situations, it's better for people not to know?

I've heard people say that the truth 'ruined' someone's life. I cannot accept such a statement. The truth offers an opportunity of living authentically and confronting reality. The truth may cause life to seem more complex than it had previously appeared, but, in actual fact, often it was the previous deceit and/or ignorance which caused the difficulties, not the revelation of the truth. Knowingly withholding the truth from someone (ie an adult) is, I believe, very insulting to them, as you are making a choice on their behalf instead of allowing them to make their own decisions. It may be difficult for you to allow your son to make his own decisions, but, as an adult, that is what he must learn to do. I hope you'll have faith in him that he will manage the outcomes.

I have met the mother of my adopted daughter and I told her that I thought she had done the right thing in giving up her child. Her action gave me the joy of raising a child and allowed me to give that child everything she needed in life. How could any mother not think that that was the right thing to do?

I don't think it's about whether it was the right thing or the wrong thing do to. If the child had a happy life does that mean that the mother did the right thing? If the child had an unhappy life does that mean that the mother did the wrong thing? It's not possible to judge the action by its consequences, as they were unknown at the time. In my opinion, the action must be judged on its motives. The mother had no way of knowing what the outcome was going to be, either for herself or for her child. For many mothers, their pain and their loss were devalued because they were being told that they were doing 'the right thing'. It may have seemed 'right' for you, but the adoption separation has had long-term implications for both your adopted daughter and her mother.

We raised three adopted children and gave them everything we could because their parents didn't want to bring them up. How can it be right for their original parents to come into our lives and try to take their children back?

It's not possible to 'take back' an adult child. Our adult children don't belong to us. Once our children reach adulthood, they form adult relationships. For adopted children, those relationships may include members of their original families. Having relationships with relatives is a normal part of life and your adult children will choose for themselves which people they wish to include in their lives. Many adopted adults have on-going contact with members of their original families, as well as members of their adoptive families. They can manage to make room for everyone if they are prepared to make the effort.

Our adopted daughter was perfectly happy and settled until her mother came back into her life. Now we never see her. This reunion has ruined our lives. Wouldn't it have been better if it hadn't happened?

It's very sad that you feel that your daughter's reunion with her mother has 'ruined' your lives. When you chose to raise another couple's child, you knew that when that child was an adult, she would develop other relationships. This is a part of growing up. Our adult children choose how much time they wish to spend with us. It seems that, at this time in her life, your adopted daughter is putting a lot of time and energy into building a relationship with her mother. It is normal for such relationships to feel all-consuming in the early stages. Is it really so hard to accept that, when you have already had all those years with her? Surely you can afford to share her a little bit now with her parents, who have never been able to spend time with her before now. As adopters, you can support your adopted daughter and show that you understand the significance for her of reconnecting with family members. Hopefully you can exhibit a spirit of generosity and concern and assist your adopted daughter to work through the issues which this reunion is raising for her. If you had a close relationship with your adopted daughter before she was reunited with her mother, then there is no reason for that closeness to be lost, just because there are now more people in her life who are important to her. I'm sure, if you are patient and understanding, this will become clear.

As an adoptive parent, I hope that they never change the legislation where we live to allow access to information to adopted adults and their parents. I think it's wrong and I've heard of so many unpleasant experiences which have resulted from adoption reunions. Don't I have a right to fight to protect my child from hurt?

Your adopted child is an adult and therefore you have no right to 'protect' your child from the truth. Your adopted child has the right to make his or her own choices. Adopted adults have been discriminated against in some places for many years by having other people make decisions on their behalf. This is quite unconscionable and must not continue. Sadly, those who claim to be 'protecting' adopted adults are sometimes acting out of their own fears and insecurities, rather than considering what is genuinely in the best interests of all concerned.

As adoptive parents, we were told that we would never hear from the original parents of our adopted children after the adoptions took place. Surely it's unfair that they have changed the rules and that parents now are making contact with their children?

Regardless of what anyone was told to expect, the fact is that the children you adopted have other families. In spite of the secrecy and denial that have taken place, all adopters know that they have chosen to raise someone else's child. All adopters know that their adopted child has other families and all adopters know that one day there could be a reunion between that child and members of his or her families. Some have chosen to anticipate and prepare themselves and the child whom they have adopted for the possibility of that event and some have not. When policies and practices are seen to be inequitable and unjust, it is right for them to be altered.

A social worker rang and told us that the mother of our adult adopted son wanted to get in touch with him. He has never expressed any interest in his families of origin and we were afraid for him in case things didn't turn out well. We told the social worker that he wasn't interested. We feel that we did what was best for him. Do you think we have any obligation to let him know?

Your son is an adult and has the right to make his own decisions. I cannot think of any other area of his life in which you would be able to make a decision on his behalf. I believe that it is only fair that he be given this information in order that he can exercise his freedom of choice and I think it is morally wrong of you to keep this from him. You also run the risk that he will find out eventually and be angry with you for taking this decision out of his hands. I also believe that the social worker acted unethically in allowing you to make this decision.

I've heard of adopted people who seek out their original families, but I'm delighted that at least my adopted daughter has a sense of loyalty to us and has told me that she would never do that. Why isn't there more encouragement for those adopted people who are loyal to the parents who raised them?

I find it a very strange definition of loyalty which would encourage adopted people not to acknowledge the truth about themselves and their places in their families. In fact I wouldn't describe that as loyalty at all. If your adopted daughter told you that she would never leave home, never marry and become independent because of her sense of loyalty to you, would you admire that kind of decision or would you consider it to be inappropriate? I know what I would think. I feel the same way about adopted people. I think that any adopter who admires adopted adults who refuse to acknowledge their origins has failed to understand the impact of adoption separation on people's lives. Agreeing to retard their emotional growth and development to please me is certainly not the sort of loyalty I would want or expect from my children. Many adopters are proud of their adopted children who seek to be reunited with their families.

When we adopted our daughter we were told that the parents were intelligent and well educated. We expected that our adopted daughter, therefore, would be a high achiever. Instead she had no interest in school and has no formal qualifications at all. When she was reunited with her mother we learned that her mother was also unskilled and that we had been deceived by the adoption agency. Would we be able to sue them for misrepresentation?

I hope that you have not judged the 'value' of your child on the basis of her educational achievements or abilities. When you adopted her, it was, presumably, because you wanted to give a child a home. As parents, we have no way of knowing what the future holds for our children, but society expects parents to cherish their children, no matter what. Parental love is expected to be unconditional and does not have to be earned. Your adopted daughter is not responsible for your disappointment. I hope that she does not sense your disappointment in her, as this could have a negative impact on her self-image.

As an adoptive parent I get tired of hearing so much talk about how important blood family is for children. We raised two adopted children and loved them more dearly than many parents who raise their own children. We always told them that they were 'special' because they were 'chosen'. Why do people make so much of the lack of blood ties and disregard the fact that it's possible to love children who are adopted just as much?

Because people emphasise the importance of family relationships, this doesn't mean that they are suggesting that relationships in adoptive families are less valuable, just that they are different. Adoptive ties don't replace family ties. They exist alongside them. Any of those ties may be weak or strong ties, but they can all be acknowledged. Of course, it's possible to love children to whom you are not related by blood. I don't believe that that has ever been questioned.

Questions asked by family members

My husband is adopted and he recently heard from his mother and father, who are now married. I didn't mind his having contact with them, but now it seems to be all he thinks about and all he talks about. I'm getting tired of it. I feel that I'm not important to him any more. Will I always have to take second place in his life?

When contact takes place between family members who have been separated by adoption, the initial emotions are often very intense and sometimes the behaviour takes on an almost obsessive appearance to those not directly involved. The feelings can be similar to those of an adolescent 'crush'. They can also resemble the feelings of grief following a death, when it seems that everything else in life is affected by the loss of the loved one. This preoccupation with the reunion, almost to the exclusion of other relationships, can last for some time, until a degree of trust is built up and the parties involved are able to reach an emotional plateau of sorts where their feelings level off. This is not to say that there won't be periods of strong emotion again from time to time, especially around particular events, like birthdays, but generally the initial intensity of the relationship does subside over time. During this period, those involved need all the support they can get from family and friends and so please try to be patient and generous. It is likely that his parents are going to continue to play a part in his life and so it might be helpful to you to read about the impact of adoption on people's lives, so that you have a better idea of the emotional turmoil your partner may be experiencing.

My mother, who gave up her first child for adoption, died of cancer when she was in her forties. She had kept in touch with some of the other mothers she had known in the home for unmarried mothers and she told me that some of them also had developed cancer. Do you think there's a connection?

I have heard that mothers who have lost a child through adoption are more likely to develop cancer in later years than other women. As far as I know there is no research to support this, but it is interesting to speculate as to whether this may have been related to their adoption separation experiences and buried grief.

My mother lost a child to adoption and she recently made contact with him. It was what she wanted and so I assumed she'd be happy when she found him. He seems to have welcomed the contact, but the whole thing has upset her so much that she's done nothing but cry ever since the reunion. She was fine before all this happened. Making contact has caused nothing but trouble. Wouldn't it have been better if she had just left it in the past where it belonged?

It may be your perception that your mother was 'fine' before making contact with her son, but, in fact, the sadness that has come to the surface now has been buried since the separation from her child. When grief is buried, it causes stress and unhappiness, although this may not have been obvious to you over the years. It can also lead to physical illnesses and may be a factor in conditions such as chronic fatigue syndrome. Giving birth to a child is never in the past; it is an experience that mothers carry with them forever and so in one sense it is always in the present. I know that there are people who say that adoption is a thing of the past and so we don't need to worry about it any more. That's like saying that polio is a thing of the past because not many people get it any more. For someone who has spent their life in a wheelchair because they had polio as a child, it is always and always will be in the present. For those whose lives have been affected by adoption separation, no matter how long ago it happened, it is always present in their lives and so for them it will never be a thing of the past. Your mother is now able to express her grief, which is actually a healthier outcome for her.

My sister got pregnant when she was a teenager and decided to give up her baby for adoption. I remember it very well. She seemed to me to have thought it all through and to be very sure that adoption was going to be the best option. She seemed quite calm about it all and believed she was acting sensibly. She never brought it up with me over the years and so I assumed that she was all right with it. Now, many years later, she's trying to tell me about her grief and suffering. She didn't look to me as if she was suffering. I'm baffled by all this talk of loss and grief. Can you help me to understand it?

While it may have appeared to you at the time that your sister was comfortable with her decision to allow her child to be adopted, for many women, the only way they could cope with what was happening, was to distance themselves from it emotionally. They presented a calm exterior because they thought that they had to go through with it and were trying to pretend that they were in control. For many of them, inside they were frightened and confused. After the birth, many mothers buried their feelings yet again, sometimes because they didn't feel that they could face them, sometimes because they thought that they were doing what was expected of them, but mostly because they felt very alone with their experience and had no idea how they should be reacting. Imagine, if you can, not only keeping your feelings inside but also then burying your experience and not even talking about it. For many mothers their hurt was eating away at them, but they were putting on a façade of being 'all right with it'. Then eventually they have the opportunity to get in touch with their feelings, to bring all that grief to the surface and to stop pretending. For many women it's like opening floodgates. All the feelings that they had suppressed over the years come to the surface, yet still those around them sometimes cannot empathise with their experience. That's why it's so important for mothers like your sister to talk with other people who have had the same experience. It would be useful for you to read about the impact of adoption on people's lives and the outcomes of suppressed grief. I hope that you can try to understand what the loss of her child has meant for your sister and to support her in her healing.

My mother has recently told us that she gave up a daughter for adoption when she was very young. I am totally shocked and cannot understand how she could have lied to us for all those years. I feel that I can never trust her again and that she is not the person that I thought I knew and loved. I am so disappointed in her, that she taught us to be honest and yet all this time she was deceiving us. She wants to try to find her daughter but I've told her that I will never accept her as part of the family and so I don't even want to hear anything about it. This has totally wrecked our family. Can you understand that I just feel devastated by the whole thing?

Obviously it's been very difficult for you to come to terms with the fact that your mother has kept this from you. I can't answer for why she thought that was best, but I do know that mothers who have lost children to adoption often agonise over keeping it a secret. Usually it's such a painful subject for them that they can't bring themselves to try to explain to other people how it happened. For many women there is a lot of guilt and shame attached to their loss and it's just too hard to bring it out into the open. When they finally do pluck up the courage to be honest and to be known for who they really are, they take the risk that others will not understand and will judge them harshly. Believe me, no one judges them more harshly than they judge themselves. The loss of a child in a family has an impact on the whole family, as you have now realised. I hope that your family can work together to heal the pain and try to talk to your mother, so that you can understand what it has been like for her. It might also be helpful if you can read about the experiences of other mothers who lost children through adoption. Up until now your mother has not been able to find the words to tell you about your sister, but now she has decided to trust you enough to share this with you. I hope that you will understand that she needs your love and support. Please don't forget that she is still the same mother that you've always known, but now she has allowed you to know her more deeply. This is one more part of who your mother is, which she has been brave enough to share with you. She will be fragile for a while as it's a very emotional time, when a mother finally reveals the loss of her child. I hope that she will be able to find support when she needs it and that she won't have to go through yet another emotional trauma alone.

A year ago, my wife met the daughter she had given up for adoption before I met her. I was delighted for her to know her child again, but now my wife is telling me that she needs to be on her own. I fear that our marriage may be over. Why has this happened, when we have been happy together for twenty-five years? I'm trying to be understanding but it seems that having her daughter come back into her life has caused the break-up of my marriage.

It's quite common for a mother who is reunited with her child to begin to question other relationships in her life. It's difficult to explain in a few words why this so often happens. Many women were deeply affected both emotionally and psychologically by the experience of being separated from their children by adoption. Often, they then embarked on relationships without having addressed those issues of loss and grief. Many women buried their pain so deeply after being separated from their children that they felt as if they were leading a false life. The constant fear of discovery also has created a great deal of tension for them. When the reunion takes place they feel such a sense of relief and, for some, they finally have permission to be true to the person that they really are. Because their relationships with themselves change, it's inevitable that some of their relationships with other people in their lives will change also. Adopted adults often go through a similar experience after reunion occurs. I'm sure your wife did not try to deceive you in any way over the years and I'm sure that you have been happy together, but now it may be for her that she is finally able to explore who she really is and cast off the mask that she feels she has been wearing since she lost her child. For some women, this experience is life-altering and, because they feel like a different person, they are no longer able to fulfil the role that they filled prior to the reunion. It may be that your wife needs some time to explore her emotions and to start to get in touch with her feelings again. I hope that you will be able to be patient and reassure her of your on-going love and support and that, in time, you and your wife will be able to resume your relationship, although it will not be exactly the same as it was before. It might be helpful if you are able to do some reading and learn more about the intensity of the emotions for women who are separated from their children by adoption and the impact on their sense of self that the reunion has.

I recently found out that my father was involved in an adoption before he married my mother. Apparently he got some girl pregnant and she gave the baby up for adoption. Now he calls this young man his son and wants me to meet him. I feel it's nothing to do with me. It's up to my father what he does, but I want nothing to do with this person. I don't even want to talk to my father about it and I wish he hadn't even told me. What do you think?

If you care for your father, then I hope that you will try to understand what this experience has meant to him. This young man is your brother (albeit half-brother) whether you choose to acknowledge that or not. It's great that your father is finally acknowledging his fatherhood and wants to include you. I hope that you'll be able to see this from your father's point of view and support him in building a relationship with his son. Your father has trusted you enough to give you a realistic picture of who he is. If you care for your father, then you'll accept him as who he really is, not who you thought he was. Your father has already suffered from having lost contact with his son and he is trying now to take responsibility for his past actions and move forward with his healing. I hope that you'll be there by his side through this difficult time and into the future.

My mother recently met the son she had given up for adoption. I'm happy for her that they have been reunited, but sometimes I know that the things he says and does hurt her. Do you think it's all right for me to talk to him about that?

I think it would be better if you talk to your mother about this issue. In the early stages of reunion, parents often find it difficult to set boundaries as they are unsure of the relationship. It takes time for a level of comfort to be reached. Your mother may need some help to deal with her own grief. Perhaps you could suggest this to her and let her manage the relationship with her son in her own way.

Many years ago my son told me that his girlfriend was expecting his child. I offered to help in any way that I could. I begged him to stand by her and help her to raise my grandchild but he refused and the baby was lost to adoption. I have never stopped thinking about my lost grandchild for all these years. Is there anything I can do to let my grandchild know that I care?

Tragically, it is seldom acknowledged that when an adoption takes place, grandparents lose a grandchild and they also can suffer from that loss. I hope that you will be able to talk to your son and encourage him to make every effort to contact his child. Perhaps if he understands that you have also suffered a loss, he will think seriously about what he can do to ease your pain and to offer, not only his care and concern, but the care and concern of his family, to his grown-up child. Meanwhile, you can contact the adoption authorities in your area or the organisation that arranged the adoption and ask if you would be able to be given any information about your lost grandchild or if they would pass on a message from you. There may be a contact register to which you could add your name. I'm sure your grandchild would be very moved to know that, even though you were not able to be involved at the time, you have carried him or her in your heart for so many years.

My wife is adopted and she suddenly decided for some reason that she wanted to try to find her parents. It's upset her adoptive parents and caused nothing but trouble. I can't understand why she started all this. She had a good upbringing, shouldn't she have left the past in the past?

It's probably hard for you to understand, but for adopted people their adoption is never in the past; it's something that will always be a part of their lives and they live with it on a day-to-day basis. Your wife didn't 'start' anything when she decided to seek out her parents. She is trying to reach a higher level of emotional well-being, find out about her families and her heritage and piece together the events of her early life. For many adopted people it's very important that they try to do that and this is a time when she could benefit from the support of those around her. It can be a difficult and emotional time and if you truly love your wife, I'm sure you'll want to be by her side as she deals with all of this. It might be helpful for you to try to learn about the impact of adoption separation on people's lives. Having had a 'good upbringing' does not mean that her family is not important to her. It's possible for adopted people to acknowledge all of their various family connections.

My wife has told me that she has heard from the son she had before we met. I knew that she had given up a child for adoption, although we never talked about it. Now she wants to meet this young man and she wants me to be with her. I've told her that he is nothing to me and that I want nothing to do with him. He's not part of my family, why should I get involved with him?

Your connection with this young man is that he is the son of the woman you love and with whom you are sharing your life. Surely you don't want to abandon her to manage this very emotional experience alone? Your wife has carried her son in her heart for many years and she wants you by her side when she meets him. I would have thought that you would have felt privileged to have been invited to share this great opportunity with her and to be able to support her and care for her as she deals with the feelings that will arise for her. Please think again and try to imagine what your wife is feeling and how you can be of help to her.

My husband is adopted and he recently obtained his original birth certificate. However he has been unable to trace his mother and the government will not help him. It's all very well giving people their birth certificates, but if people are not given any assistance to search for the other party, then what's the point?

There are very few places where official assistance is given to seek out lost family members. This is an area in which few governments feel that they have any responsibility. There are many ways of seeking people through the Internet and there are also private searchers who will try to locate family members for a fee. I suggest that you either find someone who can give you some advice on how to go about conducting a search for your husband's mother, or seek out some information on the Internet. You may also wish to try to persuade the legislators in your area to reconsider their responsibilities.

Questions asked by professionals

There are so few adoptions taking place nowadays, that I can't understand why you are still going on about post-adoption services for adult adopted people and their parents. I think we need to be putting our energies into learning from the past and using resources for family preservation purposes rather than talking about post-adoption services, don't you?

Sadly, too many people seem to think that because we have learned from the mistakes of the past and because adoption is now much less likely to be considered an appropriate outcome for families in difficulties, that there is no need to put resources and energy into providing for those who have already been separated from family members as a result of an adoption. Unfortunately, there are many damaged souls who are still suffering as a result of past adoption policies. Of course, we need to learn from the past and clearly that is happening in some places. In South Australia, for example, adoption has almost been phased out and has been replaced by outcomes which are genuinely child-centred. Just because that is happening, however, we cannot ignore the lack of services for those thousands of people who are still dealing with issues of loss and separation.

I don't see any reason why parents who gave up children for adoption should have the right to know anything about their children, once those children become adults. They gave up the right to be parents. Why should they be allowed to interfere in their adult child's life?

I have never heard of a case where a parent wanted to contact an adult child for anything other than a generous and caring reason. Presenting someone with an invitation is not interfering. Those parents lost the right to raise their children to adulthood. Once those children become adults, however, then the matter of parental rights is no longer an issue. I believe that a reunion between adopted adults and their parents allows all parties to confront their losses and experience the grieving process. This can release them from the constraints of repressed grief and allow them to move forward. Adults make their own choices in every area of their lives, but they can't make a free and informed choice if vital information is kept from them. It seems that there is a belief in the community that those parents should be condemned to some sort of lifelong punishment, by not being allowed to know anything about their own children. They often feel that society expects them to serve some kind of penance for having done what they were told at the time was best for their children. If a married couple divorce, there is no law that prevents either party from knowing about their children. Divorced parents are still parents regardless of the fact that they are no longer legally connected to each other and are actually expected to maintain a relationship with their children. When children are adopted, their parents are still their parents, regardless of the fact that they are no longer legally connected to each other. In many cases a reunion would not have taken place if the child and the parent had not both been seeking out the other. Any legislation that supports those searches is, in my opinion, a matter of social justice and is undoubtedly in the best interests of all involved.

Some people believe that any couple who would take another couple's child and pretend that it was theirs (which is what adoptive parents have done) should have been deemed unsuitable to act as surrogate parents. Do you agree?

Many years ago adoption was accepted and recognised as an appropriate way of providing homes for children who apparently had no homes. Nowadays we see things differently. I don't think it's possible to apply the wisdom and knowledge of today to times past. Community awareness and education have brought about huge social changes in recent decades, in many aspects of life. Unfortunately, there are still those who are unaware of the true meaning of adoption and there are still those who are willing to act as care-givers, only if they can have a legal document (ie an adoption order) which gives them 'ownership' of the child. I certainly would consider those people, in today's social climate, to be unsuitable to act as surrogate parents.

I find many of your comments about adoption to be offensive. I have been instrumental in arranging many adoptions throughout my life and I am proud of the number of families to whom I have been able to bring joy. What gives you the right to say that there should be no further adoptions?

Unfortunately, some people are unable to separate criticism of policies and practices from criticism of people. I do not blame those who have already been involved in adoptions. I was involved in an adoption. I didn't know any better at the time and so I don't see how I can expect that other people should have been wiser. But I do believe that we know enough now, to decide that there should be no more adoptions and I will continue to say that. For every case in which you believe that you brought joy, there was pain involved. I believe that policies and practices, which continue to create that level of pain, are unjustifiable and must be altered in the light of current knowledge. I hope that we will soon see an end to the practice of transferring children from what are deemed to be dysfunctional poor families into what too often become dysfunctional affluent families.

There are many cases where children are not safe living with their families. Sometimes those children are moved from one foster home to another. Surely they deserve the permanence and security of adoption?

Of course, those children should have some family security, but adoption, in fact, creates a sense of insecurity in children, as it suggests that family ties and relationships are not permanent and can be altered at will. A sense of identity, of knowing who they are, is often the one thing to which many damaged children cling. Feelings of safety and belonging are not created by a name change. Adoption is, in fact, designed to make them feel insecure rather than secure, because it teaches them that their identity can be discarded. Giving them a 'new' (ie false) identity suggests to them that who they actually are is unacceptable and must be hidden. The security of having a home and permanent carers can be achieved, without any alteration to their legal identity. Sadly, people talk of children 'languishing' in foster care. For me that is a dreadful expression and is very insulting to the many wonderful, caring, dedicated foster parents.

It makes foster care sound like some kind of punishment. For many children (and for many foster parents) it is a very positive, fulfilling experience. Every child is born with a mother and a father and, regardless of who raises that child, nothing can alter those relationships. A system of alternative care for children which supports that premise would actually provide children with a sense of security, in terms of acknowledging that their identity and their relationships with family members cannot be altered. If one's identity can be legally (although, of course, not actually) altered then there is no security. How can one be secure in who one is, knowing that the law may arbitrarily declare one to be someone else? I agree that children who have been removed from their families need security, but I believe that adoption does not provide that security and that better care arrangements must be created, which are genuinely in the best interests of the children. Only then will such children be able to feel safe and secure in their new homes.

Why encourage people to think of the past? Isn't it better for them to be helped to live in the present?

For those who have been separated from family members as a result of an adoption, their adoption experience is in the past, in the present and in the future. It is unconscionable for society to abandon those people simply because those adoptions happened some years ago. Our governments must be made to recognise that they have a responsibility to those who have suffered as a result of these cruel policies and practices and who now have to live with the consequences. Governments owe it to those people to do everything possible to help them to recover from the trauma created by adoption and to recover the family members from whom they have been separated by the policies of the past. Only then can they incorporate the past into the present and look forward to the future with confidence.

When you say that there should be no more adoptions, you're just talking about newborn babies being taken from their mothers, aren't you?

No. What I am saying categorically is that I do not believe that adoption is an appropriate outcome for any child, of any age, no matter what the circumstances.

It seems that in recent years the numbers of adoptions have fallen while the numbers of abortions have risen. Do you think this is a good outcome?

Adoption only becomes a possibility when there is a child who may be unable to remain and be raised with his or her family. When a live child has been born it means that there has been a sexual relationship and that conception has occurred. It also means that there has not been the use of successful contraception, that there has not been a termination (either spontaneous or medically induced) and that there has not been a stillbirth. Sexual relationships, contraception, termination and stillbirth are not issues that are caused by adoption. My topic is adoption. I leave the other issues to those who specialise in those areas.

What about children in poor countries? Don't they deserve to have better opportunities by being adopted by people in affluent countries?

There was a time in Australia, as there was in many other affluent countries, when numbers of children adopted from overseas increased as numbers of local children adopted decreased. Why did this happen? Is it because coincidentally there were correspondingly more children needing homes in other countries, as there were fewer children needing homes in countries like Australia? Or was it perhaps that, as society's attitudes changed to provide more support for children to remain with their families in countries like Australia, those who wanted children had to seek them beyond the bounds of their own countries? I'm not convinced that overseas adoptions are about caring for needy children so much as meeting the expectations of dissatisfied adults. I acknowledge that there are still issues of poverty and deprivation in some countries, but I don't think that removing children, who are the future of any nation, is in any way a solution to those problems. In fact, I believe that those who are suffering poverty and deprivation are in many cases being exploited, by those who wish to take their children from them. There is a degree of cultural arrogance at work, I think, which leads people to claim that living in an affluent, technologically advanced country is inherently 'better' than living anywhere else. There are many kinds of poverty, however. Emotional poverty can be more damaging than financial poverty. Many of those children adopted from other countries have suffered because of the separation from their families, their communities and their countries of birth. Fortunately education and awareness are increasing. I believe that countries experiencing issues of deprivation and poverty will soon put a stop to the removal of their children by politically powerful countries.

I don't understand why you seem to be so angry and bitter about adoption. It seems to have turned out all right for you. You have a good career and a good relationship with your son. Why can't you just put it all behind you now?

While it may seem to people who meet me now that I have resolved my grief associated with the separation from my son, I know how much I have suffered over the years and also how much others have suffered and are still suffering. Adoption is a subject that stirs up a great deal of emotion. I am angry at the hurt that has been caused by adoption, but I am not bitter. Anger can be a positive and productive emotion. Bitterness is only negative and destructive. I have used my experience to help others and while there are others who still need help, I hope to continue to be able to make a contribution, by educating the community about adoption and its outcomes. I know that I am very fortunate to have been reunited with my son and to enjoy a warm, close relationship with him, but I also know that there are many who are not so fortunate. I am also angry to see that adoptions are still continuing to happen in some places, as I know the difficulties that are in store for those involved. I will continue to do anything I can to reduce the likelihood of further adoptions taking place.

How would you deal with the problem of infertility? What about couples who can't have children of their own? Don't they deserve to have a child? If there were no more adoptions, how would they ever know the joy of raising a family?

Infertility is not a condition that is created by adoption. My topic is adoption. I leave the issue of infertility to those who specialise in that area. It seems astonishing to us now that, at one time, in order to be able to raise someone else's child, you had to show that you were unable to have a child of your own. How could anyone have assumed that couples who were unable to have children would be better parents than the couple who had actually created the child? In fact, raising someone else's child has its own issues, for which many adopters were unprepared. No one 'deserves' to have a child. Those who do not have children have no right to take other people's children and there are many childless people who understand this and have chosen not to adopt. To be honest, I'm horrified that anyone would even ask this question. For children who are not safe living with their families, a system of alternative care needs to be created which is honest and honours their identity. In the past, adoptions were allowed to take place because there was a lack of understanding of the value of family connections. As this understanding is now spreading throughout those countries that have previously allowed children to be adopted, the numbers of adoptions have been falling steadily. I predict that, in the near future, the wide recognition of the value of family connections will mean that there will soon be no adoptions in any country of the world. In North America, tragically, adoption has been allowed to become a business, through which practitioners earn an income. This has meant that the spread of this understanding has been hampered by financial considerations. In the United Kingdom, it appears to have been hampered simply by an unwillingness to change entrenched policies and practices, however indefensible these might be. Change will come.

Don't you think that the effects of adoption have been overstated? Isn't adoption often used as an excuse for people who are just not coping with life in general?

Adoption may help to provide an explanation for people's behaviour. I firmly believe that adoption should never be used as an excuse and I agree that, unfortunately, this does sometimes happen. I'm unhappy about the degree to which those who have been separated from family members as a result of an adoption are portrayed (and often portray themselves) as helpless victims. Adoption is often used as a justification for bitterness. Some people nurse a deep and abiding sense of resentment related to their adoption separation and they direct their energies into blaming others for perceived wrongs. I don't believe that these attitudes are helpful and, in fact, they often alienate the community in general, rather than educating and enlightening them. However, I think that for too long the impact of adoption was understated and misinterpreted and that now we have a deeper understanding of the degree of loss connected to adoption separation and the problems associated with not having grieved that loss. We still need to find ways to inform and educate our families, our communities, those in the helping professions and our politicians.

Many of those who have been separated from family members as a result of an adoption would really like to address their adoption issues, but there are no therapists or counsellors in their geographical area who specialise in adoption situations. How can they get help when there are no services available?

Some people address their adoption issues with no professional help at all and, in fact, in some situations it would be more beneficial to tackle the problem alone, than to seek assistance which turned out to be inappropriate and uninformed. Sadly, even some of the professionals and some of those employed at agencies which provide post-adoption services, are themselves ill-informed and their efforts are at best unhelpful and at worst downright dangerous. There is no doubt that good quality professional support can be very valuable. People can help themselves, however, by reading, by seeking out the support of others who have also had an adoption experience and by trusting their own instincts as to what would be useful. I also hope that they will lobby their governments and point out that they have a responsibility to provide good quality, appropriate services. They might even want to consider gaining a qualification themselves in order to be in a position to offer service to others.

Surely it can't be all right for a mother who gave up a child for adoption to be able just to ring that person up once they become an adult?

A salesperson can call that person and offer them a low-interest mortgage. If they don't want it, they can refuse that offer. So surely their mother can call them and offer them information, affection, whatever she has to offer. If they don't want it, they can refuse that offer too. That's how adults manage their affairs. They make adult choices. While I appreciate that contact with one's mother is a more serious matter than discussing mortgage options, what I am saying is, that it seems ridiculous to me that attempts are made to restrict contact between family members, when most of us accept and deal with contact from complete strangers throughout our adult lives. At least those who have been involved in adoptions have the choice to prepare themselves in advance for the possibility of contact and reunion with family members.

Your work is quite challenging and I know that you have had a huge impact on many people's lives. However, I'm sure that you have touched a nerve with some people. Have you suffered any unpleasantness from those who are jealous of your skills and insight?

Sadly, yes, I have. I feel sorry that those people seem unable to acknowledge the good work done by others and cannot see the value in working co-operatively and respectfully. I believe that their attitudes often stem from their own sense of inadequacy. However, I concentrate instead on the many warm, grateful messages which I receive from generous, honest people. I'm always happy to hear from those who appreciate my contribution and have found my work helpful.

I know of a case where a mother contacted the adult daughter she had given up for adoption, only to find that her daughter didn't know that she was adopted. The telephone call from her mother threw her into total chaos and has seriously disrupted her life and the lives of her adoptive parents. I know that you have concerns about the use of intermediaries in adoption reunions but surely in a case such as this, it would have been better to have checked with the adoptive parents first and avoided all this distress?

If distress has been caused to this young woman, let's look at who is responsible for that distress. The distress and disruption were caused by the original deceit, not by the introduction of the truth. Who is responsible for the deceit? The adopters chose to lie to the child they had adopted and knew that they were taking the risk that someone would one day reveal the truth. They are the ones who have caused the disruption and distress, not the mother. Sadly, it is becoming more and more common in our society for those who speak the truth to be blamed and for those who have lied to be defended. Frequently when there has been deceit and betrayal, which the guilty party has managed to conceal, the person who reveals the truth is castigated, while the liar is portrayed as the aggrieved party. This also happens frequently in adoption situations. I have actually heard people employed in post-adoption counselling defend adopters, who have lied to their adopted children. These workers then blame any family member who wishes for the truth to be revealed for being the cause of distress. I find it astonishing and disheartening that they cannot see that deceit is the cause of the distress and anxiety and that confronting the truth can be therapeutic. Deceit and betrayal are destructive to relationships and can never be excused or supported. In this case, the mother has done her daughter a favour by releasing her from the deceit with which she has been raised and offering her the opportunity to learn the truth and to deal with reality. I'm not surprised that the daughter is distressed and angry but I hope that she is clear about where the responsibility for that lies.

I've heard of so many bad reunion experiences. Isn't it sometimes better to let sleeping dogs lie rather than cause so much pain?

Apparently they used to tell the volunteers in the Territorial Army in Scotland that there's no such thing as bad weather, only poor preparation. In my opinion, there's no such thing as a bad adoption reunion experience, but I have heard of many cases of poor preparation. Some people find disappointment when they experience reunion, because they have allowed themselves to build up certain expectations and those are not met. Sometimes people misunderstand what has happened or can't see what has been gained from their experience. They sometimes think that the reunion has caused the pain, when in, fact, it was the original separation which caused the pain. There have been some people who have had some painful experiences following an adoption reunion, but painful experiences happen in everyone's life, sometimes as a result of adoption, sometimes not. Of course, there are risks in undertaking a reunion, but the opportunities for growth are enormous. Pain can serve a useful purpose. Sleeping dogs miss out on a lot.

Do you think it is ever a positive move to break off contact with the other party after a reunion has occurred?

First of all, I always believe that it is more advantageous for everyone that the reunion occurred than for it not to have occurred. I always advise people not to give up too easily, if there seem to be difficulties after reunion and to make every effort to resolve them. Hopefully the two parties can work out a level and a method of contact on which they can both agree. In many situations, however, regardless of whether or not there has been an adoption, there are family members who choose not to keep in touch. Sometimes that has to be accepted. There are also cases where one party has threatened, assaulted or abused a family member. In situations like these, people have to take appropriate steps to protect themselves and their family members.

There seems to be some conflict and rivalry among support groups for mothers who have lost children through adoption. I expected that mothers would support each other and work together and I have been disappointed to find that group members sometimes criticise and insult each other. Why do you think this happens?

I think that these unfortunate rivalries often occur because of jealousy and the desire for power and control. Unfortunately some mothers who were bullied into giving up their children for adoption have learned to become bullies themselves. Other mothers learned from their experience to be compliant and submissive and so they do not challenge this behaviour when it occurs in their groups. In this way insulting and bullying can become acceptable behaviour and this means that some groups take a very negative direction. Those groups generally do not survive, unless members are able to recognise what has happened and take steps to repair the damage. Ideally, group members will learn to be confident and considerate and to work together towards the same goals of supporting and educating each other and increasing community awareness of adoption issues. Support groups can be very productive, but if the members are not vigilant, they can become destructive.

What about children who were abandoned with no record of who their parents are? Can they recover from that?

It's very sad that this has happened in some cases and I believe that personal recovery can still be achieved by acknowledging and working through the impact which their circumstances have had on their lives. Some choose to seek media exposure to try to locate their families and this is sometimes successful. The challenge for all of us is not only to confront and accept what life has given us but to assess what we have made of our lives. Let us hope that support will be provided for families so that there will be no more of such cases.

I know that in most parts of Australia parents have had access to information about the children they lost to adoption, once those children are adults, for many years now. I can't imagine operating in a situation like that. How has it worked out?

It has worked extremely well and there is minimal interference from the government. It's a system that treats people respectfully and allows for self-determination. Both parents and adopted adults are considered to be responsible enough to manage their own lives and to deal with their adoption issues in their own way. There are improvements which could be made, however and I'm sure that these will occur soon. Some people handle their adoption experiences well and others do not, just as in every other aspect of life. I can't understand why those in power in other countries are so afraid of allowing people to make informed choices with regard to contact with their relatives, without placing unreasonable restrictions on them. Such restrictions would be unacceptable in any other area of their lives and I believe that they should be resisted in every way. Preventing people from obtaining important adoption information is actually in many cases limiting their opportunities for healing. I cannot see how anyone can think that that is in the best interests of the community.

In some places adopted adults and/or their parents have absolutely no right to access their adoption information. How can we make politicians understand that it's in everyone's best interests for this information to be made available?

Legislation such as this is based on irrational fear. What might help is a concerted campaign by everyone affected by adoption, adopted adults, their parents, adopters and other family members, all working together, hopefully with the support of professionals in the post-adoption field. First of all they need to educate the community (by holding public meetings, getting media coverage etc) and then there will be such an overwhelming demand from the public that politicians won't be able to hang on to those outdated ideas any longer. I think that these problems are caused by fear and ignorance. If those in power can see that the adoption community wants openness and honesty, then how can they continue to deny them that? Pointing out the fact that adoption information has been available in countries such as Australia for many years may help.

In some countries, adoption information is released only on the condition that the client attends counselling. Do you approve of this policy?

No, I certainly don't. While I appreciate that counselling can be very helpful when preparing for an adoption reunion, I object to the policy of making it compulsory. In my view this is disempowering to the client. Also, I've been told by many people that those providing the counselling are not always aware of the implications of adoption separation and reunion and may be unduly influenced by their own values and beliefs around adoption. I feel that people should be able to make informed choices about how they manage the impact that adoption separation has had on their lives, without being pressured in any way. Community education about adoption issues and the significance of reunion would help to give people more confidence in their own judgment.

What about those who never meet?

I feel very sad for those who never meet. Some have not yet met because they have chosen not to seek. Others have not yet met because, while one party feels ready, the other does not. Some have searched unsuccessfully. However, my son and I were reunited only because we were both searching for each other at the same time and so I always advise people never to give up. A degree of personal satisfaction can be obtained, by doing all in one's power to effect a reunion or to connect in some way with the other person. Some people have to be satisfied with information and, in some situations, indirect contact made via an associate. There are situations in all of our lives which we have to accept, however, because we are unable to alter them. The difficulty is in striking a balance between accepting the situation and not losing hope. It is best not to dwell to an unhealthy extent on what might have been and to be able to continue with a degree of inner peace in your life. For others the possibility of meeting has been denied them permanently because of the death of the other party. Some people who have found themselves in this situation have been able to build relationships with those who knew the deceased family member. For them at least there is a sense of finality, although it may not be the outcome for which they had hoped.

I know you think that there should be no more adoptions but some children want to be adopted. What about them?

The reason adults make decisions on behalf of children is that adults have more knowledge and more experience and so are supposed to know better. If you asked children, some of them probably wouldn't want to go to school and might prefer to stay home and watch cartoons and eat chocolate all day. Children don't understand the implications of adoption in the way that many adults do.

In some places children are removed from their parents under child protection legislation and adopted without their parents' consent. Do you agree with that?

I certainly do not. I do not believe that adoption is in the best interests of those children or their parents. I'm sure that in this day and age we can find more appropriate ways to protect our children.

Some marriages break up after reunion. Surely that can't be a good outcome for anyone?

Adoption reunions help those involved to know themselves better. Sometimes the reunion makes clear to them that they have not been living openly and honestly and obviously this has had an effect on the relationships in their lives. When they are able to get in touch with their feelings again and no longer feel that they want to hide and bury their emotions, then it often causes them to re-evaluate their relationships. For the partners of those affected by adoption separation, reunion can be a trying time. If a relationship has a firm foundation, then it will be strengthened by the self-knowledge that reunion can offer. If, however, a relationship did not have a solid footing in the first place, then this may become clear when this re-evaluation occurs. Adoption reunion is a major emotional upheaval and it is often followed by a period of adjustment.

There is so much ignorance in the community about adoption and there are so many people who try to discourage those affected from seeking a reunion. I feel that many people are put off searching by the attitudes of those around them. What can we do about this?

Confronting the truth about the place of adoption in our lives requires a degree of courage. Seeking a reunion requires a spirit of generosity. The more the community understands this, the more likely it is to happen. Unfortunately, there are influential people in governments who have the power to facilitate this understanding but, because of a combination of ignorance and fear, choose not to do so. It's our task to educate them. If adoption is talked about more openly, honestly and publicly, then the level of fear and ignorance will decrease. There are also many examples of unhelpful and unrealistic adoption scenarios in television, books and films. We can challenge these when they appear and in this way they will become less popular and less acceptable. Increasing awareness in the community of the impact of adoption in people's lives can combat these uninformed and shallow representations.

So many people's lives have been affected by adoption separation. Is there any way that they can get past their hurt and pain and find something positive about it?

Perhaps it would be helpful to present it to them in this way, 'You've had an adoption experience in your life. What have you done with it? Did you pretend it didn't happen? Did you deny it and avoid it and refuse to deal with it? Did you minimise it and pretend that it didn't mean much to you? Or did you face up to it and meet it head-on? Did you embrace it and use it as an opportunity for growth? If so, then you can be proud that you have moved past the hurt and created a positive result from the challenges which have come your way by having an adoption experience. You may now want to use your knowledge and experience to assist and inform others.'

How can people use their adoption experiences to make a positive contribution? How can they put their grief and their anger to work in a constructive way?

Those who have experienced adoption separation can help themselves and others by talking about their experiences in an informed and respectful way to anyone who will listen. In this way they can not only assist their own healing but also play their part in educating the community. We can all be instrumental in bringing adoption out into the open so that ignorance and fear will no longer prevent progress.

Conclusion

How can governments assist in the process of recovery from adoption separation?

Personal recovery

The literature on grieving and the experiences of family members who have been separated by adoption support the position that grieving a loss is a healthy, productive activity and that the suppression of grief leads to unhealthy, negative outcomes. The resolution of the grief created by an adoption loss can be assisted by the provision of a supportive environment within which personal recovery work can take place. Because adoption is a legal construction, the legislative bodies which created it have a responsibility to assist those affected to address the issues which have resulted from it.

Personal recovery will be facilitated when governments take responsibility for the outcomes of the legislation which allowed adoptions to happen. When they understand why the losses caused by adoption separation have been difficult to mourn, legislators will put in place support systems, which will assist people to perform the tasks of mourning and to achieve a degree of personal recovery. In a spirit of honesty and openness, information will also be provided to educate and inform the community about the realities of living with an adoption experience.

Funding will be provided for professional development to increase awareness among those in the helping professions, such as psychologists, social workers and doctors, about how they can provide useful support to those who are seeking to achieve personal recovery. Post-adoption support services will also be publicly funded so that informed, relevant counselling can be provided at no cost to clients.

Interpersonal recovery

An adoption is a legal arrangement. It does not change the *actual* relationships between people, only the legal rights and responsibilities. If two people marry and have a child, for example and then divorce, the legal arrangement of the marriage no longer exists but, regardless of that, each party to the marriage is still a parent to the child.

Likewise, when adoptions take place, the legal rights and responsibilities are transferred from one set of parents to another but the *actual* relationships between the parents and their children cannot be altered. Parents who lost children through adoption lost the right to raise their children to adulthood; they did not lose the right to know their children, to love their children and to offer their children the priceless gift that *absolutely no one else* can offer them - the gift of knowing the people who gave them life.

Adopted adults and their parents are entitled to make choices and decisions regarding their relationships in exactly the same way that the rest of the population does. This is not possible when vital information is withheld or when false or misleading information is provided. They have a moral right to receive full and accurate information relating to their adoption experiences.

Current legislation which involves restricting access to adoption information is based on fear. Fear of the truth is a great barrier to healing and creates a considerable degree of anxiety for those affected. *Legislation based on fear is a negative form of governance*. It does not promote honesty and health, but instead supports deceit and suffering. Such legislation encourages people to avoid reality and so healing is prevented from occurring.

Interpersonal recovery will be facilitated when adopted adults and their parents have access to their adoption information as an inalienable legal right. Family members who are seeking to achieve interpersonal recovery will be assisted when those in the helping professions learn how they can provide them with useful and appropriate support. Post-adoption support agencies will be created, which will provide search facilities to assist those seeking to locate family members and on-going support through the building of the reunion relationship. Reunion will therefore be easier to achieve and reunion relationships will also be easier to sustain.

When more and more of those whose lives have been affected by adoption have achieved both personal and interpersonal recovery, this will have a significant impact on our communities. Our legislators will learn from the experiences of those who have progressed in this way and they will use that learning to inform future social policy.

Issues which make some families unsafe, such as substance abuse, poverty, unemployment, physical and sexual abuse, homelessness and lack of parenting skills will be addressed, in order that more family homes can become the safe places they should be, in which children can grow and develop to their full potential. Family preservation programmes, which encourage and assist parents to raise their children, will take the place of adoption programmes, which create family breakdown.

Our governments will come to understand that adoption pain is not inevitable, because adoption is not inevitable. Legislation and social policy which apply to the care of children who are unable to be raised safely by their parents will be reviewed in the light of available knowledge about adoption outcomes. The result of this will be that energy and expenditure will be utilised to create a system of placements for such children, which will not produce the negative outcomes, such as maternal alienation, which have resulted from adoption.

Because of the complexities of the issues for these children, it would be appropriate for them to be entrusted to care-givers who had already had experience in raising children and who were receiving on-going professional support. As children living with chronic illness benefit from on-going medical support, so children who have had to be separated from their families will grow up with chronic emotional issues and will benefit from on-going professional support which is appropriate to their needs.

In contrast to adoption situations, which create a sense of insecurity in children by encouraging them to accept the falsehood that their adopters are actually their parents, care arrangements will be created which are safe and secure for children, without issuing a replacement birth certificate. A care arrangement which honours children's identity and history would not foster the unhealthy sense of exclusiveness and ownership in the care-givers, which has developed in many adoption situations. Our societies will demonstrate that they have learned from the mistakes of the past by accepting honest and open care arrangements which are truly designed to meet the needs of children.

I believe that these necessary changes will occur as the result of education. Those who know and understand the outcomes of adoption separation and the pathway to recovery will state their case, persistently and publicly. The result of this will be, that awareness will be increased in the community and changed community attitudes will then drive legislative change. Social action results when people decide to act on issues of which they have experience and by which they feel damaged.

These are issues of social justice. The governments which allowed adoptions to take place now have a social responsibility to fund co-ordinated, comprehensive, appropriate post-adoption services, to provide adoption information to those affected by adoption separation and to create alternatives to adoption which are genuinely child-centred.

I foresee that there will be an end to adoption in the very near future, as those who are aware continue to educate those who are not yet aware. I believe that openness and education are the most effective ways to produce this change.

How can the community assist in the process of recovery from adoption separation?

Personal recovery

There are many who have tried to work towards a personal recovery but have become discouraged by the attitudes of those around them. If you have a relationship with someone who has experienced an adoption separation, your attitude to their personal recovery could assist them towards emotional well-being. If you are a family member, a partner, an adopter, a friend or a professional, consider how you can support and assist someone who has experienced an adoption separation to resolve their grief issues and honour the truth about their experience.

In most cases, those affected by adoption separation were not able to process their grief at the time of separation, because their grief was disenfranchised. It makes it very difficult for them, if, when they try to explore this grief at a later time, they then find that they still are unable to receive community support and acknowledgement of their loss.

If the community is able to provide generous, patient support to those affected by adoption separation, to allow them to experience their feelings without judgment, then the process of personal recovery can be made easier. It is therapeutic for those who have experienced family separation to talk about their experience and it will help them if they can find a listening environment which is non-judgmental and sympathetic to their needs.

It will be helpful if members of the community, especially those in the helping professions, can inform themselves and find out as much as they can about how those affected by adoption separation might be feeling. Hopefully they can come to understand that adoption separation is a serious loss and that no matter what has happened in life subsequently, that loss remains. It is a loss which needs to be grieved and people grieve in different ways. It is important for others to remember that those who have been separated from family members by adoption have been hurt already. The best that family members, professionals and others can do is to be patient, be generous and try to make sure that *they do not add to that hurt*.

When someone decides to embark on a process of personal recovery, this may seem to require a great deal of their energy and attention for a period of time, but this will not last forever. It will be helpful if those around them can allow them to process and experience their feelings and reassure them that confronting their adoption issues is a step in the direction of emotional well-being.

Members of our communities can also be vigilant with regard to unrealistic and uninformed media reports and literary and visual representations of adoption experiences. Too often these serve to reinforce unhelpful attitudes in the community. The more those who are aware have their views represented, the more the wider community will be educated.

Interpersonal recovery

In the past, adoptions were allowed to occur because there was a lack of understanding in certain communities of the value of family connections. We are now in a much better position to understand the importance of family membership and to demonstrate our appreciation of the value of family connections.

One way that this appreciation can be demonstrated is for members of the community to be supportive and encouraging when dealing with those who are working towards reuniting with family members. If you are close to a person who has had an adoption separation experience or you are working with them in a therapeutic setting, you can help them by assuring them that you understand their search for healing and the part played in that search by reunion.

Adoption has traditionally been steeped in secrecy. Parents have often kept their lost child a secret out of fear of being criticised (especially by those closest to them) and adopted people have often thought of their families in secret because they feared withdrawal of love from their adopters. Later in life, some do not share their search and reunion experiences with those close to them, as they fear negative responses. *Keeping a secret is often about fear of not being loved.* If those who are seeking reunion do not receive reassurance from those around them, they may choose to deal with these issues alone. Because the experience of reunion can be a very emotional one, however, it could be very helpful to them to have the support of those close to them.

For those who are living with an adoption secret, it may be helpful if you consider that not sharing your adoption information with others may not be about fear of how it will affect them, but, in fact, about fear of how it will affect your relationship with them. Those who have been separated from family members by adoption often have a strong need to please others and to retain their approval. It takes courage to be honest and to be able to accept that how other people react to you is about who they are and not about who you are.

Otherwise, what you may be doing is withholding from those close to you the opportunity to know you more completely and preventing them from having an experience which will allow them to grow, develop and adapt. You are not, in fact, being kind to them or to yourself. You are permitting yourself and others to be affected by deceit, which can place more of a strain on a relationship than the truth would. If you are able to be honest, then the relationship can move forward on the basis of *reality*, not *pretence*.

Adopted people sometimes say that they are afraid to tell their adopters that a reunion has occurred in case their adopters are ‘hurt’ by the news. In fact, I believe that what they often fear is a withdrawal or withholding of affection as a punishment by the adopters. Adopted people often feel insecure in both families, as the ties that bind them to the adoptive family do not include heredity and the ties that bind them to the original family do not include personal history. Because of this, both positions feel, to a degree, unsafe. Sometimes, therefore, adopted adults are unwilling to put themselves further at risk of exclusion. Many adopters, however, are delighted when their adopted children are reunited with family members. They see the reunion as evidence that their adopted children have a healthy awareness of the significance of their identity and are working towards personal and interpersonal recovery.

Experiencing an adoption reunion changes the way the participants feel about themselves and so it will also often change the way that they relate to those close to them. An adoption reunion allows the participants to know themselves better, to live more authentically and to be known for who they really are. They may have been living, to some extent, a sort of shadowy existence prior to the reunion, because they have been living with ignorance, fear or pretence. After the reunion has occurred, however, they are more able to accept themselves for who they are and to expect others to do likewise. This may present a significant challenge to those close to them.

Sometimes relationships break down as a result of this and sometimes they are strengthened. For a relationship which was founded on fear of exposure, the future was always fragile. In either event the relationship is able to be conducted more honestly.

How can individuals help themselves in the process of recovery from adoption separation?

Personal Recovery

This book has been written about and for those who, like me, have been separated from a family member by adoption. For us, adoption is a given. It has already happened. Our challenge is - W*hat do we make of the impact of adoption in our lives?* How can we live in such a way that we honour ourselves and our adoption experiences and celebrate our family relationships?

Those of us who were separated from our children through adoption were usually told that we should put the experience behind us and go on with our lives as if it had not happened. Those who were adopted were often told that they should consider themselves to be part of their adoptive families just as if they were born to those families. Many of those affected by adoption separation, therefore, did not understand that this separation was an experience of loss from which they may find it difficult to recover. Attempts at addressing recovery issues were frequently viewed by those not affected as self-indulgent and unnecessary. It is important first of all, therefore, to understand and acknowledge that recovery from an adoption separation is an appropriate and valuable goal.

Once that understanding has been reached, we can then begin to work towards that recovery. I do not feel that it is helpful to try to assess whether or not we have reached a position of complete recovery. It is likely that our recovery will be a lifelong experience in which success is difficult, if not impossible, to measure. However, I believe that making an effort to achieve personal recovery following an adoption separation will benefit everyone involved.

There are those whose lives have been affected by adoption without their knowledge. For example, there are cases in which a child has been adopted and not told the truth about his or her personal history. There are also situations in which parents are unaware that they have lost a child through adoption. Some mothers were told that their babies had died. Many fathers were not made aware of the birth of their child. For those people, discovering the truth, no matter how long after the event, gives them the opportunity to learn from their adoption experience. It is never too late to learn.

There are ways in which we can take advantage of the learning opportunities which adoption has provided for us. These are some suggestions, not placed in order of importance. This list is by no means exhaustive.

~ Imagine, regardless of your religious beliefs, that, when your life is over, you will have an opportunity to account for the way in which you have faced the challenges and opportunities for growth which your life has brought you. Suppose that you could be asked what you have learned from those challenges and if you have used your learning to help others. Anyone who plays cards knows that winning is a combination of the cards which are dealt and the skill with which they are played. There are cards which we have been dealt in life, over which we had no control, but there are choices which we are able to make now. Try to imagine how you would account for your use of time and opportunities throughout your life. If you had to account for your life choices, would you be satisfied with what you have achieved and contributed?

~ Explore how you feel about adoption. Then, rather than considering whether your feelings are right or wrong, think in terms of whether or not they are useful to you and are helping you towards your goal of personal recovery. Try to assess whether or not your feelings are appropriate and helpful. You may not be able consciously to change how you feel, but you may be able to use your feelings productively rather than destructively.

~ Focus on your strengths. What skills and strategies have you already used to address your adoption issues? If you are adopted, you have grown up having to adapt to unusual family circumstances. If you are a parent, you have had to accommodate the loss of your child into your life somehow. How can you use the strengths which you have already demonstrated to help yourself and others to progress through life in a positive direction?
~ Find something positive about your adoption experience. Adoption in our lives is not a punishment, nor a curse. It is an opportunity. As parents, we sometimes feel that the only way we can remember our child is to remember our hurt. We associate the child with the pain. It sometimes saddens our children if they feel that all they represent to us is misery. For their sake and for our own we can try to learn what can be gained from our experience. Perhaps in order to move on from our pain we can find something positive in the existence of our child, so that the child is not inextricably linked with pain and loss forever. It is important not to allow the pain of the past to spoil the pleasure of the present. If you are adopted, rather than thinking about what you have missed in your life, focus on the people who have loved you and cared about you.
~ Take ownership of your adoption experience. It is your loss, your experience and is unique to you. How are you going to incorporate it into your life? Will it make you bitter and sad or can you gain some benefit from it? Prepare yourself to share your experience with others in a powerful way that does not allow them to make you feel ashamed and inferior. We have been through something that other people have not. How has it altered us? How can we grow from our loss?
~ If you think that you are an inferior person in some way, either because you were adopted or because you lost a child through adoption, is there evidence of that in your life? Test your feelings against the reality. Look at yourself honestly and focus on your achievements and admirable qualities.

~ Rather than focussing on what you have lost through your adoption experience, think of what you can give as a result of it. How has adoption made a contribution to your life and how can you use your experience to make a contribution to the lives of others? Our adoption experience can help us to have compassion for the tribulations of others and to put life's other challenges into perspective.

~ Think about what you have done with your adoption experience. Have you used it as a stick with which to beat yourself? Have you used it as an excuse for your failure to achieve your goals? Have you transformed it into destructive bitterness and used it to blame and accuse others? Or have you looked at what you could gain from it? Has it made you more resilient? Has it given you a deeper understanding of yourself, of other people, of life itself?

For most people, pursuing personal recovery leads them on to seek interpersonal recovery. There are some, however, who have not yet been able to achieve a reunion. For them, a great deal of healing and inner peace can still be achieved through personal recovery.

Interpersonal Recovery

There are many, however, who do proceed from personal recovery to interpersonal recovery. Many of those who have understood that they have suffered a loss and have accomplished a degree of grieving for that loss are then able to summon the courage and generosity, either to seek out lost family members or to respond to any lost family member who has contacted them. In this way they are able to invest energy in restoring lost relationships.

There are strategies which can be used, to help us to take full advantage of the learning opportunities which the reunion experience can provide for us. These are suggestions only and are not placed in order of importance. This list is by no means exhaustive.

~ Remember that people are often prepared to work at a relationship, such as a marriage, for many years. An adoption reunion also needs to be worked at and it is well worth the effort of being prepared to continue that work for many years.
~ Try to communicate honestly. One person's perception of the situation may be quite different from the other person's. For example, the mother may believe that she is making the child feel welcome in the family by issuing frequent invitations to family events. The child may interpret her behaviour as smothering or demanding. It will be helpful if people communicate honestly rather than act on their own perceptions and perhaps withdraw suddenly from the relationship, leaving the other person devastated and unable to understand the reasons for their behaviour.
~ Deceit between adults can be corrosive to a relationship. If one party decides to keep information from another party in the belief that they are 'protecting' them, what they are actually doing is preventing them from having an experience which they could use for growth and learning.
~ It is important to distinguish between facts and perceptions. Rejection is a perception but not necessarily a motive or intention. After reunion some people interpret the other person's behaviour as rejection or abandonment but people rarely describe their own behaviour in that way.
~ Be aware that the other party may have formed close attachments in the time which you have spent apart. It will not be helpful to your efforts to build a relationship, if you do not acknowledge the importance of those ties.
~ Try to have the courage to accept the truth which the other person is offering you and the generosity to offer your truth to the other.
~ Reunion is not about obligation. Adult children and their parents don't owe each other anything. Reunion can, however, be about courage, generosity and opportunity.

~ Try to appreciate all the positive aspects of the reunion relationship. It is sad when people do not allow themselves to enjoy what they have, just because it is only good but not perfect.
~ Sometimes it seems that the reunion takes both parties back to the time of the original separation, when neither of them felt that they had control over the situation. The result of this is sometimes that both the parent and the child want to exercise control at the time of reunion. Such a struggle for power can make life difficult for everyone. Be aware of this and try to be accommodating.
~ It is important that you feel confident to be yourself in the relationship. If you try to conform to the expectations which you believe the other party has of you, this could lead to disappointment and confusion in the future.
~ People are not responsible for other people's happiness. People are also not responsible if they cause disappointment to others. We must take responsibility for our own expectations. You cannot change the other person's behaviour but you can change how you feel about it. You are responsible for finding your own peace, regardless of the other party's behaviour.
~ Keep in mind that the other party may have had no preparation at all for this event. While this does not excuse rudeness and unpleasantness, it may explain inappropriate comments and tactless statements. Be prepared to be patient and to allow the other person to learn and understand.
~ Rather than focussing on what you hope to gain from the reunion, think about what you have to offer.
~ If you are hoping that the other party will exhibit respect, honesty and acceptance, then make sure that you are demonstrating those qualities yourself.
~ Try to strike a balance between looking after your own well-being and trying to empathise with the other person. The growth of the relationship will depend very much on both the quality and quantity of the interactions between the parties. Even when there is distance involved, interactions can be warm and meaningful.

~ For parents, with the children we have raised, we have seen them as helpless infants and watched them grow and struggle through childhood. We have adored and admired them as they learned how to walk, talk and become independent. It is so much easier for us, later in life, to tolerate their difficult times and their unhappy moments because we have those warm, sweet memories to sustain us. With the children we have not raised, however, it is more difficult, as we did not know them when they were dependent, innocent children. We did not share their learning experiences and receive their hand-made gifts and expressions of love. For adopted people, they may have watched the adopters who raised them face challenges and make sacrifices. They may have shared close moments with them and have been on the receiving end of tolerance and support when times were difficult. When they meet their parents, however, they have no such memories upon which they can call. It takes time to build a 'new' relationship and so it is not helpful to compare that relationship with other family relationships, which have a quite different background.

~ Someone may request that you do not write to them or call them but they have no more right to expect that you will comply with their request in an adoption relationship than anyone else would have, where there was no adoption involved. When you decide whether or not to comply with their request, think of the long term outcomes. What is your goal? If you want to have a relationship with the person which is on-going, what is the best way to go about that? Only you can decide.

~ Be cautious and remember that you are dealing with a damaged person, who has most likely never gone through an experience quite like this before and who is learning, perhaps by their mistakes. Please reassure this person that you care about them and admire them for taking the steps that they have taken already and that you can be patient and generous, while they prepare themselves to take further steps into the unknown.

~ The two parties involved in the relationship, eg a mother and son, have to create their unique mother/son relationship. There is no question of whether or not it is going to be a mother/son relationship. That is what it is and nothing can change that. But there are as many types of mother/son relationships as there are families in the world and only one particular mother and son can work out the parameters of their relationship. There is no set way that a mother and son will relate to each other and will behave together, regardless of whether they have spent the developing years together or not.

~ There is sometimes a strong attraction between family members who have been separated by adoption. I feel that it relates to the fact that we, who have lost a close family member, seem to place a keener importance than usual on those who reflect ourselves in some way. Parents may subconsciously search for their missing child in other people that they meet. If they meet someone who reminds them of how they were in their youth, they may think that this could be their lost child. Adopted people may spend their lives living with people who do not reflect them, either physically or in their personality and so they seek someone who does. Adopted people, in fact, are often attracted to partners who resemble them. When they then find someone who does genuinely reflect them, either in appearance, tastes or mannerisms, they tend to be very drawn to that person. Be aware that this attraction can occur, although it rarely causes serious problems in a relationship. The intensity of the physical attraction usually reduces to a manageable level over time. If there are on-going issues with attraction then it may be wise to seek professional support.

For many it is only after reunion that the true nature of their adoption loss becomes apparent. For many years it seemed to me that becoming pregnant at the age of nineteen had 'ruined my life'. Since meeting my son, however, I have gradually come to the conclusion that holding on to that view might have a negative impact both on my relationship with him and on my personal healing. I have reconsidered that position and have decided that in honour of my son and my love for him, I am now able to take a different view. If I had continued to take that stance then it would have meant that my first experience of motherhood had been for me a negative one.

Instead I have been able to examine the positive aspects of my experience and the ways in which I have used it to develop my potential. This has involved not only improving my own skills but also assisting others. I now recognise that every child is a gift, not just to their parents, but to the world. I have tried to use my loss and my sadness to develop my understanding of the experiences and emotions of others. I have tried to use my grief to help me to appreciate the joy in my life and to bring a degree of peace to the lives of others.

For those of us who have already been involved in adoptions, our challenge is, how can we all - parents, adopted people, adopters and professionals - ensure that our lives have not been *diminished* by our involvement with adoption? Parents can do it by honouring and acknowledging their parenthood. Adopted people can do it by developing the best elements of their nature and their nurture. Adopters can do it by acknowledging the contribution they have made in raising the child of other parents. Professionals can do it by supporting practice and policy which will help to heal the pain and avoid more pain in the future. We can all do it by appreciating the uniqueness of our adoption experiences and acknowledging the extent to which we have used those experiences as opportunities for personal growth.

A magnificent pearl is created as a result of the intrusion of a grain of sand into an oyster shell.
We can choose what we create from the intrusion of adoption into our lives.

A Message from the Author

I recently re-read one of my favourite books, *Narziss and Goldmund*, by Herman Hesse. In it, Hesse tells the story of two men, whose friendship began in their youth and lasted until death, in spite of the different directions taken by them throughout their lives. Narziss spent his life in intellectual and spiritual pursuits, in seclusion, as a scholar and a monk. Goldmund passed many years in physical and romantic pursuits, travelling, having adventures and avoiding commitment. Their friendship was characterised by acceptance, concern and loyalty.

Goldmund found that he had a talent for woodcarving and, when he was reunited with Narziss after they had spent some years apart, he created a wooden statue of the Madonna for the abbey of which Narziss had become Abbott. Its beauty and depth were much admired. Goldmund explained to Narziss, *To shape that figure it needed the whole of my youth, it needed all my vagrancy and loves, and every woman I ever knew. That is the source of my work.*

I have been able, in recent years, to develop my skills as a counsellor, a writer and a speaker. In each of those areas I have drawn on my experiences in life, especially the adoption of my son and my reunion with him. I, too, have taken risks in my life. I have travelled and had adventures. I have experienced many interesting and moving events and relationships, which have, to some extent, been the source of my work. I believe that I have created much that is very worthwhile out of the variety of life events and interactions of which I have been a part.

I have been fortunate in my life to have had my share of both tears and smiles. It gives me great personal satisfaction to use what I have experienced to enrich the lives of others and to help them to heal.

Evelyn Robinson, March 2004

About the author

Evelyn Robinson, MA, Grad Dip Ed, BSW, has both personal and professional experience of adoption separation and reunion. Evelyn gave birth to her son, Stephen, in Edinburgh, Scotland, in 1970 and he was adopted soon after his birth. Stephen and Evelyn were reunited in 1991 in Australia and continue to enjoy a close relationship. Evelyn has also been a professional social worker since 1996 and has been employed since that time as a counsellor and educator in the post-adoption field. She has always given generously of her time and energy to promote healing for those who have been separated by adoption and to educate the community around the long term outcomes of adoption separation. Evelyn has travelled within Australia and to New Zealand, the United Kingdom, Ireland, Canada and the United States, in her own time and at her own expense, providing training and information sessions to members of the adoption community, professionals, government departments and adoption support organisations. She has also presented conference papers on adoption-related topics in some of these locations and in Romania and South Korea. Her books inform the work of professionals around the world and are used as self-help manuals by those who have experienced adoption separation. While each person's response to an adoption separation is individual, some general exploration and understanding of the issues can be useful to everyone. Even when there has been no adoption, many adults suffer from separation losses and find themselves considering a meeting with someone with whom they have a genealogical connection. Evelyn's books are also for them. Through her international presentations and her books, Evelyn has made an enormous contribution to increasing awareness around the world of Australia's enlightened approach to adoption separation and reunion, now widely respected and admired. Evelyn was appointed in September, 2009 to the National Inter Country Adoption Advisory Group which meets with the Australian Attorney-General's Department, to advise on intercountry adoption policy and practice. Further information about Evelyn Robinson and her valuable work is available from www.clovapublications.com.

CPSIA information can be obtained
at www.ICGtesting.com
Printed in the USA
LVOW12s1011140417
530876LV00001B/13/P

9 780987 193117